THE CTSO
COMPETITION
COMPANION

THE CTSO
COMPETITION
COMPANION

Your Competition Authority

RACHAEL MANN

This book is dedicated to Jason Garcia, 2013 FCCLA Culinary State Champion, C-CAP Award Winner, and the Art Institute "Chopped" Scholarship Recipient. Jason was an example of the transformational impact of Career and Technical Student Organizations and an inspiration to those who crossed paths with him. He left this world too quickly and his memories will live on.

TABLE OF CONTENTS

ABOUT THE AUTHOR

 Rachael Mann is the founder of #TeachlikeTED and coauthor of the Amazon best seller, *The Martians in Your Classroom*, and *The Spaces You'll Go*. She speaks and writes about the future of work, and what these advances mean for education. Rachael is a TEDx speaker and coach, a Google Certified Educator, and has a master's degree in Educational Leadership. She is a founding member of the Council on the Future of Education where she collaborates with global experts to create educational change.

As a former DECA chapter president, adviser, judge, and state director, Rachael understands CTSOs AND teens. Rachael is a sought after national keynote speaker with a message designed to engage and entertain, while simultaneously educating youth on the projected changes in the world around us, and steps to take to be successful and have a competitive edge.

"...how you do anything is how you do everything."
~ SIMON SINEK

Introduction

WHAT IS THE CTSO COMPETITION COMPANION?

Your first guess may be that this book will help you win Career and Technical Student Organization (CTSO) competitions, and while that is one of the primary objectives, I have a much larger intent in offering this information (cue dramatic foreshadowing music here!).

Everyone wants to be a winner. Why else is it standard practice to hand out trophies to every young child on a sports team, regardless of their athletic merit? But what happens after the win? It is a bit underwhelming in that you are now the proud owner of a cheap gold-painted plastic mockery of what once symbolized true greatness—just like every other person on the team.

Even if you win a trophy that is not based on mere participation, you will also learn that while winning a competition may be a phenomenal feeling, it is also fleeting. 2. This CTSO competition companion offers more than a few tips on how to win a competition or two. This book is your authoritative resource on how to win... at life. No more gold painted flecks to dust off of your shoulder, because living life big is the big win. As self-development author Simon Sinek reminded us in the opening quote "... how you do anything is how you do everything." and true greatness requires practice, so let's begin!

WHY CTSO?

What does Taylor Swift, Troy Aikman, Jay Leno, Courtney Cox, and Mark Zuckerberg have in common? Aside from enjoying the perks of having a spotlight on them, they were also members of a CTSO when they were in high school. Will a CTSO guarantee your own personal assistants and paparazzi? Perhaps! But even if that is not how you choose for your life path to unfold, your CTSO will help you build skills that will open doors and opportunities that may have never been possible otherwise.

Just think, Taylor Swift learned how to *shake it off,* Troy Aikman learned to excel as a *team player,* Jay Leno learned that a *sense of humor* can win over almost anyone, Courtney Cox mastered networking and making *friends,* and Mark Zuckerberg discovered the game changing formula for *getting likes and followers.*

So what skill sets will CTSO help you master? The sky is no longer the limit!

Though competitions may vary from CTSO to CTSO, there are common threads that apply to all of the competitions, no matter which one you decide to pursue.

The truth is, competitions can be scary (… really scary!). There are too many unknowns. If you have competed before, you most likely woke up on the morning of your competition (…assuming you were able to get some sleep!) and found yourself wishing you had just one more week, one more day, or heck—even one more hour—to prepare.

This book was written to address those fears so you can get restful sleep the night before, wake up refreshed, hit the ground running and ready to show the world, or at least your judges, your best self.

While this book was written as a comprehensive guide for students and members of the CTSO, it will also become an invaluable tool for advisers and family to help support your efforts throughout your competition journey.

WHAT QUESTIONS WILL BE ANSWERED IN YOUR CTSO COMPANION?

In this book, you will learn how to make your presentation or demonstration become the dynamic bar that is set for future competitions, how to communicate effectively, and how to prepare for the day of the competition. You will also learn why there is more to your competition than just winning. Most importantly, this book will leave you better equipped to be your best self when it matters most. *The CTSO Competition Companion* will address:

- How do I select the competitive event that is best suited for me?
- How can I best prepare for this event?

- Who is my competition?
- Who are these judges (...and why are they so intimidating?)
- Why didn't I win first place?
- I won my state competition, what's next?
- How do I handle the anxiety I feel?
- How do I improve my communication skills (...so the judges understand how brilliant I truly am?)
- How can I prepare for the unknown variables and predict the worst case scenarios?
- How can I make an unforgettable first impression?
- And more!

HOW TO USE THIS GUIDE

Stand-Alone-Chapters

This book is designed in a stand-alone chapter format, so you may read this book from cover-to-cover, or skip around to the chapters that you feel are most relevant in the moment. Also, please feel free to make this book your own by making notes, adding post-its, highlighting the heck out of it, and doodling whatever your creative heart desires. By doing so, this companion becomes your friend (...a bestie—if you will!) throughout your journey and like any bestie, this will be the one you will remember to revisit often for future events.

Guest Voices

Throughout this guide, you'll find advice, tricks, and tips from former CTSO competitors, advisers, and judges who volunteered to drop in and share their expertise in order to help you on your journey to competition readiness. They have even kindly agreed to share their contact information, so be sure to reach out and connect with them directly.

Resources

You'll find TONS of tips, links, and references, and resources throughout this guide that will help you succeed. Be sure to use them to your advantage.

YOYO

At the end of each chapter or section, you will find a section called, YOYO (You're On Your Own)! This area will provide you with prompts for reflections for journaling or questions to ponder and then answer, along with an additional area for your own notes. Use this space to create a map of your exciting journey, or if you prefer—you can use a separate notebook or space on your own digital device to record your responses.

Remember—this is YOUR competition journey! YOU determine your level of success (...and I just know... YOU are going to do great!).

If you want to find the real competition, just look in the mirror. After awhile you'll see your rivals scrambling for second place."

~ **CRISS JAMI**

Chapter 1

WHAT EXACTLY ARE CTSOS AND WHY DO THEY MATTER?

According to the National Coordinating Council for Career and Technical Student Organizations (NCC-CTSO) "Career and Technical Student Organizations (CTSO) enhance student learning through contextual instruction, leadership, and personal development, applied learning and real-world application. CTSOs work as an integral component of the classroom curriculum and instruction, building upon employability and career skills and concepts through the application and engagement of students in hands-on demonstrations and real life and/or work experiences through a Career and Technical Education (CTE) program. CTSOs help guide students in developing a career path, a program of study and provide opportunities in gaining the skills and abilities needed to be successful in those careers through CTSO activities, programs and competitive events. In addition, students have opportunities to hold leadership positions at the local, state, and national level and attend leadership development conferences to network with other students as well as business and industry partners."

In a nutshell, CTSOs provide students with an opportunity to develop as an individual, connect with others, and open doors for experiences that wouldn't necessarily be available otherwise. CTSOs are the keys to learning how to be a leader, provide a service to the community, to plan events, win a competition, and yes... Win at life too!

 Chapter Incentive Program—Frequently Asked Questions...
http://nmctso.com/chapter-incentive-program-frequently-asked-questions/
http://www.ctsos.org/wp-content/uploads/2019/03/2016-Final-Definition-NCC-CTS-JULY-16.pdf

WHAT SETS CTSOS APART FROM OTHER STUDENT ORGANIZATIONS?

What each CTSO shares is that each event is aligned to program areas and to focus on each area's specific academic skills, employability skills, and technical skills which ultimately strengthens career readiness. All CTSOs have competitions that involve public speaking components, skills demonstrations, product creation, written projects, recognition events, and knowledge tests. All CTSO competitive events require advanced preparation, deadlines, judges, and opportunities to advance to national or international competitions. But each CTSO is unique and different from each other, and different from clubs that may be offered.

First, let's look at how CTSOs differ from clubs, and then we will take a peek at what makes your CTSO different and unique from the others under the CTSO umbrella. Frequently, CTSOs get lumped in with clubs and other school related activities, however there are some important distinctions. First, CTSOs are connected to a CTE class and are intra-curricular. This means that what's happening in the classroom is supported in the CTSO and the two are sometimes so intertwined, which means you may hear students refer to their agriculture class as their FFA class, or their marketing class as DECA, and so on. This also means that the CTSO is deeply connected with a career path, whereas an organization like Spanish or Chess club, most likely isn't designed to prepare it's members for a specific career. CTSOs also have officer positions, meetings, a constitution, and bylaws while clubs may not have each of these components. Finally, CTSOs are recognized at the national level and have specific guidelines to govern its structure.

> *"CTSOs, such as SkillsUSA provide skills-based competitions for students… based largely on students' abilities to work individually or in teams to solve problems and present projects to judges from industry and education… They clearly support student mastery of the "STEM competencies," as many problem—or project-based learning experiences do."*
>
> **~ JULIE SILARD KANTOR**

WHAT MAKES MY CTSO UNIQUE?

While the Office of Vocational and Adult Education (OVAE) lists eleven student organizations, here are eight CTSOs that are officially recognized by the National Coordinating Council for Career and Technical Student Organizations (NCC-CTSO).

Other organizations that are widely recognized are included in the sections that follow. While there are many similarities and offerings within organizations sometimes overlap, each CTSO has a unique focus and structure.

The NCC-CTSO recognized organizations are:

- Business Professionals of America (BPA)
- DECA
- Family, Career and Community Leaders of America (FCCLA)
- Future Business Leaders of America | Phi Beta Lambda (FBLA–PBL)
- Health Occupations Students of America (HOSA)
- National FFA Organization (FFA)
- SkillsUSA
- Technology Student Association (TSA)

https://www.acteonline.org/wp-content/uploads/2018/03/CTSO_Career_Readiness.pdf
http://www.ctsos.org/

 FUN FACT:

"Most readers probably know that an **acronym** is an invented word made up of the initial letters or syllables of other words, like NASA or NATO. Fewer probably know that an **initialism** is a type of acronym that cannot be pronounced as a word, but must be read, letter-by-letter, like FBI or UCLA."
https://www.dailywritingtips.com/acronym-vs-initialism/

Let's take a brief look at each of the CTSOs and please remember to also visit your state and national websites for more information about your organization and competitive events.

BUSINESS PROFESSIONALS OF AMERICA (BPA)

Business Professionals of America is the nation's leading CTSO (Career and Technical Student Organization) for students pursuing careers in business management, information technology, finance, accounting office administration, and other business-related career fields. With 45,000 members in over 1,800 chapters across 25 states and Puerto Rico, BPA is a co-curricular organization that supports business and information technology educators by offering co-curricular exercises based on national standards. BPA is dedicated to the preparation of a world-class workforce through the advancement of leadership, citizenship, academic and technological skills.

Throughout the fall, winter and early spring, Business Professionals of America State Associations hold Fall, Regional and State Leadership conferences for leadership development, competitions, awards, elections and more.

Some BPA conferences consist of all divisions together at a single conference, whereas some BPA states hold conferences for their divisions separately. Additionally, some states have a fall and winter/spring conference, while others only hold a winter/spring conference.

To learn more about the national competition, visit https://bpa.org/nic.
Calendar—Business Professionals of America.
https://bpa.org/events/calendar/
Our Mission and Vision—Business Professionals of America.
https://bpa.org/about-us/our-mission-and-vision/

DECA

DECA's competitive events are aligned with the career clusters of marketing, business management, administration, finance, hospitality, and tourism. Each event has a written component and an interactive component. Industry professionals serve as the judges in this event.

Visit DECA's website and access the amazing resources that are made available to members, including competition advice through DECA Direct Online, Sample Role-Play Presentations, the Exam Blueprint, and a link to a slide deck that explains what penalty points are and how to avoid them.

https://www.deca.org

FAMILY, CAREER AND COMMUNITY LEADERS OF AMERICA (FCCLA)

FCCLA has been around since 1945 and was originally called Future Homemakers of America. In 1999, the organization rebranded and became FCCLA, which stands for Family, Career, and Community Leaders of America. Family as its central focus. The mission of this student organization is to promote personal growth and leadership development through the stages of life.

The competitive events are open to high school students and include the Knowledge Matters Virtual Business Challenge, LifeSmarts Knowledge Bowl, Skill Demonstration Events, and STAR events. For resources and templates related to FCCLA competitive events, visit the program tab on the national FCCLA website and go to competitive events: http://fcclainc.org/programs/competitive-events.php

GUEST VOICE: CODY HAYS
President of Cody Hays Multimedia Management
www.codyhays.com

The Secret to Taking Home the Gold In FCCLA
What makes FCCLA competitions so unique?

When you join FCCLA, you're joining more than just another career and technical student organization. You're joining a family. FCCLA is the only CTSO with family as its main focus, and this really shines through in how the organization conducts their competitions. In FCCLA competitions are called STAR Events, standing for Students Taking Action with Recognition. Members are recognized for proficiency and achievement in chapter and individual projects, leadership skills, and career preparation.

FCCLA falls within four career clusters: human services, hospitality and tourism, education and training, and visual arts and design.

Competitions include Life Event Planning, Chapter Review, Culinary Arts, Teach and Train, Interior Design, and more. Competitive event selection is relevant to a students career cluster.

In FCCLA there is a unique scoring system. Each student or team's presentation is assessed by a panel of industry judges and ranked from 0 to 100 based on a scoring rubric provided by FCCLA. There is no clear first, second, third place—rather, gold, silver, and bronze medal winners. Depending on the team's score, they can achieve a certain level of award. Anyone who scores 90 points or above receives gold, anyone who scores between 80 and 89 points achieves silver, and anyone 70 to 79 points achieves bronze. At the state level, it is typically the top two scores that qualify for nationals, regardless of whether they achieved gold, silver, or bronze status.

Want to excel in your competition?

In order to excel in any competition, you'll want to focus on storytelling and creating an interactive experience for your judges. Yes, it's definitely important to reference your scoring rubric to ensure that you're going to hit all the topics the judges are looking for but understand that no judge wants to just sit and be talked to. They have 10 other competitors doing the same thing—what's going to make yours so unique? Think outside the box… get creative with your presentation and share your message like you would tell a story.

My junior year of high school I competed in Chapter in Review Display. I covered a four-foot-tall by one-and-a-half-foot wide tube with a map and put the tube on a lazy-Suzan which gave it the ability to spin in a circle. I put our chapter photos on the tube and told our Our Chapter's Journey, and gave the judges a peek into our road trip of a year. We started out at the first day of school, made a pit stop for lunch at the Annual Farmer's Market, and continued our journey through the hills and valleys of our year, finally ending up at the State Leadership Conference with a spot to place a photo… "our journey was not over yet!" Along the way, I stopped to check in and ask questions of the judges to get them invested in my presentation—don't be afraid to make impromptu comments and jokes if your judges are reacting to what you're talking about! This engages your judges and breaks down the wall.

PS—I ended up getting gold and qualifying for nationals and I definitely know you can too!

FUTURE BUSINESS LEADERS OF AMERICA | PHI BETA LAMBDA (FBLA–PBL)

The FBLA competitive events are referred to as the National Awards Program and is designed to recognize and reward excellence in business and career-related areas. Students must compete at the state level and be eligible to compete for national awards in order to advance. States are able to modify the events that are offered, so be sure to check with your state guidelines.

At the State Leadership Conferences, students compete in events testing their business knowledge and skills. Top state winners are then eligible to compete for national awards at the National Leadership Conference each summer. States may modify the events offered at the district/region and state level. Always check your state guidelines if competing at the district/region and/or state level competition.

FBLA provides a flow-chart to help members select an event that is a fit. This link shows the 2018 chart, however, check the website to find the latest and most relevant version.

https://www.fbla-pbl.org/media/Choosing-your-FBLA-competi-tive-event-2018.pdf

 To explore the events that are available to you along with competition guidelines visit, https://www.fbla-pbl.org/fbla/competitive-events/guidelines/
FBLA Competitive Events: Academic Competitions for High...
https://www.fbla-pbl.org/fbla/competitive-events/

NATIONAL FFA ORGANIZATION (FFA)

Formerly Future Farmers of America, FFA is the largest CTSO with close to 670,000 members and a presence in all 50 states, Puerto Rico, and the Virgin Islands. Middle school, high school, and college students are eligible to be apart of this organization. Skill development and career preparation are central to FFA's competitive events. At the national level, competitions are in 50 areas. At the local and state levels, recognition is given through proficiency awards in the areas of Entrepreneurship, Placement, Combined, and Agriscience research.

"The letters "FFA" stand for Future Farmers of America. These letters are a part of our history and our heritage that will never change. But FFA is not just for students who want to be production farmers; FFA also welcomes members who aspire to careers as teachers, doctors, scientists, business owners and more. For this reason, the name of the organization was updated in 1988 after a vote of national convention delegates to reflect the growing diversity and new opportunities in the industry of agriculture." https://www.ffa.org/about-us/what-is-ffa/

Another opportunity for members is the National FFA Agriscience Fair which is for middle school and high school students interested in science and research. Members compete at the local level and are able to advance to state and national levels.

 Agriscience Fair | National FFA Organization Agriscience Fair. https://www.ffa.org/participate/awards/agriscience-fair/ Career and Leadership Development Events | National FFA... https://www.ffa.org/participate/cde-lde/

HEALTH OCCUPATIONS STUDENTS OF AMERICA (HOSA)

HOSA was created for students interested in pursuing a career in health care and supports these future health professionals. The program is designed to motivate and recognize students as they develop skill competencies that are integral to Health Science Education.

"HOSA is not a club to which a few students in school join. Rather, HOSA is a powerful instructional tool that works best when it is integrated into the HSE and health science related curriculum and classroom." http://www.hosa.org/about

HOSA competitive events reward and recognize members who have the determination and commitment to pursue excellence.

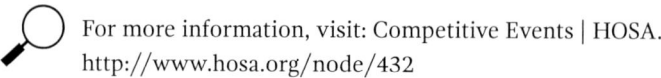 For more information, visit: Competitive Events | HOSA.
http://www.hosa.org/node/432

NATIONAL YOUNG FARMER EDUCATIONAL ASSOCIATION (NYFEA)

NYFEA is a diverse organization with membership covering the entire spectrum of agriculture. NYFEA is the only national organization specifically dedicated to the next generation of young agriculturalists. The purpose of NYFEA is to develop leaders, inspire service, strengthen communities, and enhance the success potential for American agriculture, especially the beginning farmers.

Agriculture's Promise (Washington Experience):

NYFEA has discovered a bounty of opportunity. From visits to the historically significant and extremely motivational monuments to the discussions with key policy makers at both USDA and in Congress, the attendees have found this to be an extraordinary experience. All organizations with an emphasis group (council, committee, advisory board...) focusing on training and encouraging the next generation are invited to attend. All that is required is a willingness to join in the group policy discussion. This event is hosted at the headquarters hotel and coordinated by NYFEA. Otherwise, individuals and groups are encouraged to canvas "the hill" and share their story of why the United States must make a commitment to the next generation of agricultural leaders, better access to credit, good rural leadership support (easy access to the dollars), added funding for collegiate scholarships for rural young people, etc. This event is in the Spring of each year.

 To learn more about the events offered by NYFEA, simply click this link: http://www.nyfea.org/institute-brochure. Membership—NYFEA. http://www.nyfea.org/membership.html

NATIONAL POSTSECONDARY AGRICULTURAL STUDENT (PAS) ORGANIZATION

The National Professional Agricultural Student Organization (PAS) is a student-led organization that allows students to build and sharpen their skills so that they are ready for the workplace. Through competitive style learning and real-life application, our members are skilled professionals and prepared to work in all areas of the agriculture industry.

PAS is one of the 11 career and technical student organizations that has been approved by the U. S. Department of Education as an integral part of career and technical education.

For nearly forty years, PAS has been developing two and four-year college-level professional agriculture students for the workplace through participation in employment experience programs, skill-set development, network opportunities, and organizational activities.

It's one-of-a-kind national collegiate-level competition-style learning model gives students the practical and hands-on development opportunities essential for career success. Students compete at the local, state, and national levels and are guided by faculty advisors to develop the technical, professional and soft skills required for career success within the agriculture industry.

 For more information on the competitive events that PAS offiers visit their site at: https://www.nationalpas.org/events www.nationalpas.org. https://www.nationalpas.org/

SKILLSUSA

The philosophy of the Championships is to reward students for excellence, to involve industry in directly evaluating student performance and to keep training relevant to employers' needs. In 2018, over 6,500 members competed in 103 separate events.

SkillsUSA covers the largest number of career areas out of all of the student organizations. The competitive events are referred to as the SkillsUSA Championships. Students have the opportunity to compete locally, regionally, at the state level, and then to advance on to the national levels.

Visit https://www.skillsusa.org/competitions/skillsusa-championships/contest-descriptions/ for brief descriptions of all of the SkillsUSA Championship competitions. This will help to narrow down which competitions may potentially be a fit for you. From there, visit the SkillsUSA Championships Technical Skills and read the official rules for each event that you have selected. For new competitions, you will find a link at the end of each contest description.

GUEST VOICE: KEVIN J FLEMING, PH.D.
Vice President of Strategic Development, Norco College
www.KevinJFleming.com

How SkillsUSA Provides you a Competitive Advantage

The SkillsUSA Framework emphasizes personal, workplace, and technical skills which prepare every student to achieve career success. This framework is valuable in overcoming two major obstacles that we face in the 21st century. First, our skilled labor gap.

We know that the most difficult-to-fill vacancies are for skilled workers. This is because the true ratio of jobs in our economy is 1:2:7. This means that for every occupation that requires a master's degree or more, two professional jobs require a university degree, and there are over half a dozen jobs requiring a 1-year certificate or 2-year degree; and each of these technicians are in great demand. Yet, according to recent surveys, more than 33 percent of employers have unfilled job openings. They simply can't find applicants with the necessary skills. These are good-paying jobs, too. In fact, Harvard Business School found that 27 percent of trained skilled professionals earn more than the average bachelor's degree recipient! Success in today's world depends on aligning a student's career with their skills and available job opportunities. Yet there is growing evidence of a skills-gap in which many Americans are not receiving the hands-on training that is needed.

The true ratio of jobs in our economy is 1:2:7. https://www.linkedin.com/pulse/true-ratio-jobs-our-economy-127-steve-gratz

The second obstacle we face is Career Readiness. When asked to rate the importance of applied skills to high school and college graduates' successful entry-level job performance, employers overwhelmingly report consistent responses across all three educational levels. Research shows that most students are graduating deficient in teamwork, collaboration, professionalism and work ethic. These most frequently reported applied skills considered "very important" by industry also include oral and written communication, social responsibility, critical thinking and problem solving. Fortunately, there is hope!

In response to these two obstacles, SkillsUSA has created a Framework that helps students showcase technical skills, to connect you to employers, and to teach employability skills that are validated by in-demand industries. SkillsUSA changes the trajectory of student's lives by enables them to articulate to employers what skills they have developed and how that will benefit their potential employer.

The first of three components is Personal Skills. These include a student's work ethic, professionalism, sense of responsibility, and self-motivation. Second is Workplace Skills which focuses on teamwork, communication, decision making, and leadership. The third framework component is Technical Skills Grounded in Academics. These include areas such as computer and technology literacy, service orientation, safety and health. This trifecta of student success has been validated by multiple sources and research studies. The Framework centers on industry demand and builds the foundation for relevant, intentional student learning and leadership development.

SkillsUSA not only benefits students to develop a rich skill set, meet employer's needs, and provide true career readiness for students engaged in local chapters. It also a) provides experiences and opportunities to compete locally, regionally, and nationally, b) it benefits teachers and your school's Career & Technical Education (CTE) programs to further provide a quality workforce for your community, and c) SkillsUSA is a significant part of the solution to shrinking our national skills gap.

In SkillsUSA's history (over 50 years), over 13 million students have participated and been empowered to become world-class workers, leaders, and responsible American citizens. Gain a competitive advantage and check out joining, or starting, a SkillsUSA chapter at your school.

TECHNOLOGY STUDENT ASSOCIATION (TSA)

Not to be confused with Transportation Security Administration, the Technology Student Association (TSA) enhances personal development, leadership, and career opportunities in science, technology, engineering, and math (STEM), whereby members apply and integrate these concepts through intra-curricular activities, competitions, and related programs. TSA accelerates the achievement of its members through engaging opportunities to develop STEM skills. TSA provides opportunities at the middle school and high school levels.

The competitions that TSA offers include categories such as Biotechnology Design, Career Prep, Coding,, Leadership Strategies, Medical Technology, Prepared Presentation, Software Development, Technology Problem Solving, Video Game Design, Webmaster, and much more.

 To learn more about the competitions and events offered by TSA, click this link: https://tsaweb.org/competitions-programs/tsa/high-school-competitions
TSA Story—tsaweb.org. https://tsaweb.org/about/about-tsa/story

OTHER STUDENT ORGANIZATIONS

At the state level, you may find additional ones that are not listed here, but that are recognized as student organizations, such as ROTC and Thespians. Be sure to visit your state CTSO website and talk to counselors to find out more about what is recognized in your state. One that is commonly recognized is Educators Rising, which we will explore below.

EDUCATORS RISING (EDRISING)

Formerly called Future Educators Association (FEA), the purpose of Educators Rising is to guide students through the process of becoming teachers. The organization provides support to high school and college students, and early career professionals.

Educators Rising offers 20 national competitions as of 2019. The events and awards are organized into the following categories: Secondary Level, Post-Secondary Level, and Professional Level Awards. Be sure to find out the guidelines for your state to determine if you need to first compete at the state level in order to advance to nationals.

 For more information on Educator Rising competitions, visit https://www.educatorsrising.org/what-we-offer/competitions.

YOYO
(YOU'RE ON YOUR OWN)

In this chapter, we explored the different CTSOs. What CTSO are you involved in? How is it similar to other CTSOs?

_____

_____

_____

_____

What makes your student organization unique?

_____

_____

_____

_____

Involvement in a student organization becomes a huge part of the memories you make in high school and becomes a part of your identity. What do you identify most with in your CTSO? In other words, what do you like about the CTSO(s) that you are a member of? What makes you proud to be apart of this CTSO?

_____

_____

_____

_____

Visit the state and national websites for your CTSO. What resources are available that will help you as you prepare for your competitions? List the resources here and bookmark the links on your digital device.

_____

_____

_____

_____

Create a free Wakelet account by visiting www.wakelet.com. Once you have created your account, create a collection for CTSO resources. Later on in your competition readiness journey, you will add an additional collection(s) to keep track of all of your artifacts that are related to your competitive event(s).

_____

_____

_____

_____

Competition to catalyze digital innovation is great. Competition to further the world of pursuing superego is unhealthy."

~ PEARL ZHU

Chapter 2

WHY COMPETE?

There are tons of reasons for taking your CTSO membership to the next level and by entering in one of the competitive events. The opportunity to gain entrepreneurial and leadership skills while still in high school through access to CTSOs and competition readiness will ultimately give you a competitive edge in life. This chapter will explore the numerous reasons for you to compete and illustrate how preparing to compete and then engaging in the competition itself will transform your life and open countless new opportunities. But first, let's hear from a North Dakota CTE Director, Eric Ripley.

GUEST VOICE: ERIC RIPLEY

Executive Director of Career & Technical Education
Grand Forks Public Schools
Grand Forks Area Career & Technology Center

Why Should Students Compete in CTSOs?

CTSOs are a critical component of any Career & Technical Education program, providing the students leadership opportunities, a sense of connection with the school, completion of service projects, networking with other members, and of course, the ability to compete in CTSO competitions. Competing within a state or national leadership conference may be the attribute of CTSOs that are the most recognizable by students, advisors, schools, parents, and community members as you can probably envision the pictures of the awards stage, with winning students proudly displaying their medals and trophies.

I would argue that while the end result for some will be to don a winning medal, all students that choose to compete in CTSOs are in fact successful. Successful in demonstrating their knowledge and skills gained within their CTE program, successful in placing themselves in a competitive environment against a group of their peers, and successful in positively representing their school and organization. A famous quote by Joe Torre reads, "Competing is not about winning. It's about preparation, courage, understanding, and heart. Winning is the result." There is an internal pride in showcasing one's abilities, to put forth one's best effort in an event that aligns with one's career interests. It is the preparation for and experience of competing that makes all CTSO students winners.

WHY COMPETE? *IS YOUR NAME ON THE LEADERBOARD?*

In a Harvard Business Review article entitled, "We Wait Too Long to Train Our Leaders, Jack Zenger shares the following:

> *"When I looked back at our database of some 17,000 world-wide leaders participating in our training program, who hailed from companies in virtually every sector throughout the world, I found that their average age was 42. More than half were between 36 and 49. Less than 10% were under 30; less than 5% were under 27.*
>
> *But the average age of supervisors in these firms was 33. In fact, the typical individual in these companies became a supervisor around age 30 and remained in that role for nine years —that is, until age 39. It follows then, that if they're not entering leadership training programs until they're 42, they are getting no leadership training at all as supervisors. And they're operating within the company untrained, on average, for over a decade.*
>
> *Practicing anything mildly important, like say skiing or golf, without training is inadvisable. The fact that so many of your managers are practicing leadership without training should alarm you."*

Strong leadership is the one ship that is guaranteed to keep your head above water. So go ahead! Throw that life jacket out—because you've got your own back when you are a leader. (*...um. Just kidding—we don't really throw life jackets away! I was just testing you to see if you are still paying attention!*)

Are you wondering if you have the leadership skills you need? You are certainly off to a good start! How do I know? You had to acquire several skill sets along the way through your engagement in CTSO functions, social events, charity events, and chapter meetings—but I bet you didn't know you were learning these skills—did you? Even competitive events that are not categorized specifically as leadership competitions are constructed by utilizing skills that include project management, public speaking, time management, and teamwork. This means you are always developing and demonstrating these skills sets, which offers you a huge advantage over your peers as you move forward in your life. So take what you already know as the leader (...that perhaps you never even knew you were!)... and start adding more opportunities to grow as a leader as a focused effort to help you with your competition, and in all areas of your life.

WHY COMPETE? PROFESSIONAL DEVELOPMENT

In order to compete, you will most likely attend a conference and in addition to your competition, you will likely have other opportunities. Don't skip out on the keynote presenters, breakout sessions, and demos. It is important to learn from the experts at the event because then you will have a one-of-a-kind experience under your belt (...or in the pocket of your hoodie, or under your hat) that most people do not encounter until many years further down their career path!

WHY COMPETE? NETWORKING

Connecting with business and industry thought leaders through vendors, sponsors, politicians, college representatives and other business professionals is another important experience gained throughout the events. So, don't be shy and look everyone in the eye and introduce yourself. Repeat his or her name when it is spoken and give them a firm shake any time the opportunity presents itself.

> *"The conference is filled also with corporations smart enough to get in the door early and meet the best and brightest of our country. These kids all come out of high school with a TANGIBLE SKILL and are ready to work impressive attitude. THE COMMON DENOMINATOR = RELEVANCY."*
> **~ JULIE SILARD KANTOR**

More than just connecting with the adults at the event, network with CTSO members from different chapters and even different content areas. Get to know as many people as you can—you never know when your paths will cross again! That gal from law and public safety may be pulling off to the side of the road to check on you when you have a flat tire on the highway. The student in the cosmetology class? Yep, you guessed it! Make a habit of building positive and respectful relationships with everyone who crosses your path.

WHY COMPETE? EXPLORE POTENTIAL CAREER PATHS

Each CTSO competitive event is created with the correspon-
ding career paths in mind. The time and effort that you put into
preparing for your event will help you determine if this is an
area that you are merely interested in or if it should become
your passionate pursuit. In addition, career exploration is just
as much about determining a bad fit as it is about determining
the right one. *(Or to put it more simply, these competitions give
you a chance to casually date a particular field of interest before you
decide to put a ring on it.)*

As a culinary arts teacher, I had a student who participated in
multiple culinary related competitions through FCCLA as well
as through community events and C-CAP. Towards the end of
her second year in the program, she came to me and asked if
we could talk. She wanted me to know that she had decided
to pursue a degree in the field of Early Childhood Education
instead of Culinary. She seemed shocked and relieved when I
told her that this was wonderful news. She thought this news
would disappoint me, but as an educator I genuinely want students to follow their own path—not mine. I was genuinely happy
that her hard work had paid off. She had not only won several
competitions, but also developed excellent culinary skills and
other transferable skills, while narrowing down which career
path which was the best fit for her.

On the other hand, most of my students who participated in
CTSO competitions were happy to learn that the competition

he or she chose, ignited their passion in that field, regardless of whether they won the medal.

Participating in regional, state, national, and international competitions is a fantastic addition to your resume. The recipient of your resume, job, or college application will immediately recognize the determination, commitment, and tenacity you illustrated in your competitive event.

YOYO
(YOU'RE ON YOUR OWN)

Journal

Reflect on the leadership skills that were mentioned in this chapter. What skills do you already have from your previous experiences?

_____

_____

_____

_____

What are three leadership skills that you would like to develop through your competition(s)?

_____

_____

_____

_____

As you prepare for your competitions, think about the career paths that are related to your chosen event(s). What are they?

_____

_____

_____

_____

Are these competitions related to a career that you could see yourself in one day?

_____

_____

_____

_____

Bookmark this page and return here after you have completed your competitions.

How did you do?

_____

_____

Did your level of interest in the related career paths increase, or decrease, or stay the same?

_____

_____

How can you showcase your newly acquired expertise with real examples? Do you have service projects and community events? Chapter recognition? Individual or team wins?

_____

_____

_____

_____

Use this space to clarify your purpose, cause, or belief that inspired you to register for the CTSO competition.

_____

_____

_____

_____

Why Ask Why?

Do you have your answer? It is important in life to ask "why?" when you embark on any endeavor, this one included. Knowing the answer to this question will drive you through the coming months and headed straight toward competition success!

_____

_____

_____

_____

What is your biggest motivator for competing?

_____

_____

_____

_____

What are your secondary motivators?

_____

_____

_____

_____

How do you hope to benefit from your CTSO competitions?

_____

_____

_____

_____

How much time are you willing to commit?

_____

_____

_____

_____

Who will you need assistance from?

_____

_____

_____

_____

Self Assessment

Read over the following skill sets to determine how you rank in professionalism by using a scale of 1-5, with 5 being the score that illustrates you are without a doubt absolutely perfect in that characteristic. To learn more about this topic, you can visit the creators of this chart at Kent University by clicking here: https://www.kent.ac.uk/ces/sk/skillstest.html

WRITTEN COMMUNICATION

- Thinking through in advance what you want to say .... ① ② ③ ④ ⑤

- Report Writing Skills .... ① ② ③ ④ ⑤

- Gathering, analysing and arranging data in a logical sequence .... ① ② ③ ④ ⑤

- Developing your argument in a logical way .... ① ② ③ ④ ⑤

- Briefly summarize the content .... ① ② ③ ④ ⑤

- Adopting your writing style for different audiences .... ① ② ③ ④ ⑤

- Avoiding jargon .... ① ② ③ ④ ⑤

NEGOTIATING AND PLANNING

- Developing a line of reasoned argument ... ① ② ③ ④ ⑤

- Emphasising the positive aspects of your argument .... ① ② ③ ④ ⑤

- Understanding the needs of the person
  you are dealing with .... ① ② ③ ④ ⑤

- Using tact and diplomacy .... ① ② ③ ④ ⑤

- Handling objections to your arguments .... ① ② ③ ④ ⑤

- Making concessions to reach agreement ... ① ② ③ ④ ⑤

- Challenging the points of view expressed
  by others .... ① ② ③ ④ ⑤

VERBAL COMMUNICATION

- Accurately hearing what people are saying .. ① ② ③ ④ ⑤

- Able to clarify and summarise what they
  are communicating .... ① ② ③ ④ ⑤

- Being sensitive to their values and feelings .. ① ② ③ ④ ⑤

- Not interrupting .... ① ② ③ ④ ⑤

- Helping others to define their problems .... ① ② ③ ④ ⑤

- Telephone Skills (thinking through in
  advance what you want to say. Keeping
  business calls to the point.) .... ① ② ③ ④ ⑤

- Making a speech (thinking up an interesting
  way to put across your message, structuring
  your presentation, using audio-visual aids
  effectively, successfully building a rapport
  with your audience.) .... ① ② ③ ④ ⑤

- Body language .... ① ② ③ ④ ⑤

COOPERATING OR GROUP WORK

- Contributing your own ideas effectively
  in a group .... ① ② ③ ④ ⑤

- Taking a share of the responsibility
  in a group .... ① ② ③ ④ ⑤

- Being assertive—rather than passive or
  aggressive .... ① ② ③ ④ ⑤

- Accepting and learning from constructive
  criticism and giving positive, constructive
  feedback to others .... ① ② ③ ④ ⑤

- Concentrating on behaviour that can
  be improved .... ① ② ③ ④ ⑤

- Identifying your strengths and weaknesses .. ① ② ③ ④ ⑤

INVESTIGATING AND ANALYZING

- Clarifying the nature of a problem before
  deciding what action to take .... ① ② ③ ④ ⑤

- Collecting, collating, classifying and
  summarising data .... ① ② ③ ④ ⑤

- Being able to use results effectively using
  text/graphs/tables/pictures .... ① ② ③ ④ ⑤

- Finding where the required information
  is available .... ① ② ③ ④ ⑤

- Gathering information systematically .... ① ② ③ ④ ⑤

- Formulating questions .... ① ② ③ ④ ⑤
- Being able to condense information/
  produce summary notes .... ① ② ③ ④ ⑤

LEADERSHIP

- Setting objectives .... ① ② ③ ④ ⑤
- Organising and motivating others .... ① ② ③ ④ ⑤
- Taking the initiative .... ① ② ③ ④ ⑤
- Persevering when things are not
  working out .... ① ② ③ ④ ⑤
- Taking a positive attitude to
  frustration/failure .... ① ② ③ ④ ⑤
- Accepting responsibility for
  mistakes/wrong decisions .... ① ② ③ ④ ⑤
- Being flexible—prepared to adapt goals
  in the light of changing situations .... ① ② ③ ④ ⑤

PLANNING AND ORGANIZING

- Managing your time effectively/using
  action planning skills .... ① ② ③ ④ ⑤
- Prioritising tasks effectively .... ① ② ③ ④ ⑤
- Setting objectives which are achievable
  and measurable .... ① ② ③ ④ ⑤

- Identifying the steps needed to
  achieve goals .... ① ② ③ ④ ⑤

- Using lists .... ① ② ③ ④ ⑤

- Being able to work effectively under
  pressure/managing stress .... ① ② ③ ④ ⑤

NUMBERS

- Use simple statistics .... ① ② ③ ④ ⑤

- Calculate percentages .... ① ② ③ ④ ⑤

- Multiply and divide accurately .... ① ② ③ ④ ⑤

- Read and interpret graphs and tables .... ① ② ③ ④ ⑤

- Use a calculator .... ① ② ③ ④ ⑤

- Managing a limited budget .... ① ② ③ ④ ⑤

"In any moment of decision, the best thing you can do is the right thing, the next best thing is the wrong thing, and the worst thing you can do— is nothing."

~ THEODORE ROOSEVELT

Chapter 3

WHICH EVENT SHOULD I COMPETE IN?

You know you want to compete, but how will you choose from so many exciting competitions? Each CTSO varies in numbers of nationally and state recognized events.

When deciding whether to go for an event that is also a national event or in your state only, you need to take into consideration if you are going to be available and willing to go to nationals. If nationals are important to you, you may want to focus all of your energy on events that will get you there. However; if you know that you are not available on the dates of the nationals, or unable to travel to the event, that doesn't mean that events that lead to nationals are off the table. If the event that is the best fit for you happens to fit in this category, go into the competition with the same enthusiasm and give it your best shot. Once you have won your competition, let the organizers know right away that you will not be able to compete at the next level so that they can pass the opportunity on to the next highest qualifying entry.

State level events have many benefits which include scholarships to local schools, monetary prizes, local/state recognition.

"Make a decision. It doesn't have to be a wise decision or a perfect one. Just make one."

~ SETH GODIN

STAY IN YOUR LANE OR MERGE?

Do you have a driver's license? If so, then you already know what happens when you try to drive fast in the slow lane or drive slow in the fast lane—not only is it bad for you, but it puts others in a compromised position as well. Or what if you are accustomed to driving in the desert but then suddenly you find yourself somewhere with snow covered roads? Staying in your own lane is important in driving... and in competitions! What does this mean? In this case, it means that you should stick with something that you are good at. It also means that you will need to determine in advance if you are at your best when performing as an individual, or if you work better with a partner or a team as most CTSO's have competitions that fall into each of these categories.

In some cases, getting out of your lane and your comfort zone can be a really good thing. If it's something that you are interested in, passionate about, and you are willing and able to invest the time into "merging" into that lane, then by all means, this is your opportunity to explore new horizons and develop new skills while acquiring new knowledge that may open more doors for you in the future, and may lead to a successful competition.

> ### 💡 TIP:
>
> Does your organization have a guide to help you determine which competition is a fit?
>
> For example, DECA offers a chart to help guide members to the best potential competition https://www.deca.org/wp-content/uploads/2018/07/CE_Poster.pdf

Take some time to review the competitions that are offered through your CTSO and then narrow these options down to 5-10 events that are in your wheelhouse AND that you would enjoy competing in.

Next, reread the descriptions for each competition. Is there anything that disqualifies you from competing? If you are considering registering for a team event, do you have someone who qualifies that would join you? After you have narrowed it down to events that you are eligible for, what events are you interested in?

You may also want to take into consideration the popularity of an event. Are you able to find out how many usually compete in this event? Although an overly popular event doesn't exclude it, you have to work even harder to stand out. See chapter 12 for more on this.

Remember, competitions are updated yearly. Be sure to check your CTSO website for the most current information and graphic organizers.

IS THAT YOUR FINAL ANSWER?

Being able to make decisions and then make those same decisions work is a key component to building a successful strategy for life. Sometimes it means not looking back or second guessing if it was, in fact, the best decision. When it comes to competitive events, in most cases, it's best to commit to your decision, and then make the most of it. Don't spend so much time trying to decide on the perfect competition for you, that you end up losing the precious time that you could have spent preparing for the competition. Spending too much time pouring over the competition descriptions can also lead to decision fatigue, which could lead to not competing at all. Don't let that happen to you!

> *"Go ahead and act as if your decisions are temporary. Because they are. Be bold, make mistakes, learn a lesson, and fix what doesn't work. No sweat, no need to hyperventilate."*
>
> **~ SETH GODIN**

YOYO
(YOU'RE ON YOUR OWN)

Work through these questions to help narrow down the event that is right for you.

Do a realistic assessment of your time commitments and available time to prepare for a competitive event. How much time can you commit on a daily basis? Weekly? When is the competition date? How much time can you commit between now and then? As you read through competition descriptions and requirements, assess if it is something that you are able to dedicate enough time in order to meet the competition demands.

Breakdown of Time

Daily	Days Until Competition	Daily x Days until Competition = Time Dedicated to Preparing for event

---

Do you enjoy the adrenaline rush of real-time challenges and thinking on your feet or do you prefer situations that provide an opportunity to rehearse and prepare in advance?

_____

_____

_____

_____

Are you at your best when you are preparing individually or working with a partner or in a team?

_____

_____

_____

_____

Do you prefer to be able to submit results in writing? Take a test? Submit a project or product? Or do you prefer to be able to demonstrate or explain your work?

_____

_____

_____

_____

Determining the answers to these questions will help you to find the competition(s) that are the best match for you. Find the competitions that match your responses.

"It's much easier to be convincing if you care about your topic. Figure out what's important to you about your message and speak from the heart."

~ NICHOLAS BOOTHMAN

Chapter 4

PARTNER EVENTS AND TEAM EVENTS

"Talent wins games, but teamwork and intelligence wins championships."

~ MICHAEL JORDAN

Competing with a partner or in a team provides an opportunity to develop skills that are important in almost every career: teamwork and collaboration. That being said, it's important to approach your preparation and execution in a deliberate manner. I have witnessed first hand more than just competitions falling apart, but also friendships ending in a fall out due to not approaching the preparation in a way that set everyone involved up for success. It's important to plan for a successful event that results in deepened relationships and feeling good about the contributions that each person has made towards a successful competition.

For partner and team events, work through the following:

1. What is your plan for preparing for the event? Create a plan, including a timeline and a chart of responsibilities.
2. Establish norms for collaboration, communication, and for avoiding conflict.
3. Decide how you will handle hard conversations. What if a team member misses a deadline? A meeting? Doesn't show up on the day of the competition?
4. Have a system of accountability along with a tool to track progress. Tools such as Trello, Workboard, shared calendars, shared docs, etc will help you to create a system that works for everyone.
5. How will you collaborate? Take advantage of tools such as Google Hangout to ensure that you are meeting and collaborating regularly, even when it's not face to face.
6. Score each other anonymously using a google form to find out how others in your group feel the distribution of labor is panning out. This also adds a layer of accountability. Make sure all group members are on board for trying this one, it could have the opposite effect if it isn't a group decision and some are not on board.
7. Know the Guidelines for team events. If a team member doesn't show, can you have a substitute? Can you compete without the individual?
8. Be sure to have multiple chapter members check and recheck the entry and materials before submitting anything.
9. If presenting about your entry, and multiple people will be speaking, keep in mind any time restrictions. Ensure that you

have rehearsed this and do not go over or under the allotted time.

10. Know each other's part, whether it's spoken word, a demo, or any other component. Be ready to step in and help your team member out if needed.

YOYO
(YOU'RE ON YOUR OWN)

Work through each of the tips listed in this chapter with your team and come up with a game plan for each. Are there some areas that are of greater concern than others?

_____

_____

_____

_____

Explore tools for organization and for collaboration that you and your partner or team will use. What are they? Make sure that each person feels comfortable with the chosen platform(s).

_____

_____

_____

_____

What will you personally commit to doing to ensure that this will be a positive experience in which your relationships will grow as you join in on this effort together?

_____

_____

_____

_____

"Google realized that great minds weren't the key to their success. It was great teams that created a connection where their minds were free to create great inventions."

~ JON GORDON

Chapter 5

WRITTEN WORD: APPLICATIONS AND RESUMES

Most competitive events will involve a written component, including the application to compete and submitting a professional resume. Here are some tips to ensure that your "written word" puts you at the top of the stack rather than eliminating you from making it to the next stage of the competition.

Unlike speaking to someone face-to-face where body language, inflexion, tone of voice, and facial expressions add to the actual words that are being spoken, written word is not as forgiving of mistakes. If you say something wrong when talking to someone, you have an opportunity to recover or sense from the other person's response that you haven't provided enough information or need to lighten the tone. For written word, it is even more important to take into consideration the audience and to get feedback from multiple people to ensure that your final draft will make a lasting impression.

GRAMMAR COUNTS!

Nothing spoils a resume or application like a typo, except for an unprofessional email address. I remember scoring a stack of FBLA applications and resumes. When a resume came through with something along the lines of yournexthotty@gmail.com, it landed in the bottom of the stack... of my recycling bin... (I am only slightly exaggerating...)

GUEST VOICE: DANNY RUBIN
The Resume

How to make any competition, internship, or job look remarkable

Based on an excerpt from Danny Rubin's ACTE-supported book, Wait, How Do I Write This Email?

You may think your experiences, internship or job is nothing special or, better yet, a stepping stone to an actual career. You may even believe, "Who wants to learn about my boring job? I should play up my work ethic and personality instead." So your resume ends up full of words like hard worker, team player, dependable.

That line of thinking is wrong. Wrong. Wrong. Wrong. (have I mentioned wrong?)

Don't Save the Drama for Your Mama
You can make any job, no matter how mundane, leap off of the page. Doing so all begins with one question: Where's the drama?

A Brief Example:

Let's say a fictional woman named Shannon Jones has a job filing papers and answering phones at a medical practice. Maybe this isn't the job she wanted to pursue for 30 years, but this is where she landed (...and again—she's fictional—so fortunately we don't have to waste our tears on her mispent adult life in a job she didn't want with a husband who doesn't love her... but alas, I digress.).

So perhaps the work experience on this sad fictional character's resume may say:

Answer phones and provide customer service at a medical office.
Assist people with concerns in a friendly and courteous manner.
File patient paperwork and help to keep the office organized.

So where's the drama? How can we save Shannon? What can we do to add sizzle to a passionless job she never wanted and help her get a new one?

What about this?

Answered 75 to 100 phone calls a day at one of the busiest medical practices in Houston.
Checked in 50–60 patients each day and often work with three to four people at the same time.
Helped manage files for nearly 2,700 patients and digitize critical medical information.

See what I mean? Do you feel the drama now?

Checking in 50–60 patients each day while working with three to four people at a time is far more interesting than someone who assisted people's concerns in a friendly and courteous manner (SNORE!).

Now the employer pictures the applicant hustling while keeping order in a hectic doctor's office. This woman is cool under pressure, doesn't get rattled, and handles the stress—like a boss!

The two job descriptions sound like different people, don't they? (...So perhaps since we are getting her a new job, and a new attitude, we can now give her a new fictional husband too! One she is crazy about who supports her new career! ...but again—I digress.).

So...how can you add drama to YOUR resume?

Ask yourself how were your jobs or internships dramatic ...or at least challenging? What made each day tense or stressful?

Then, bring those moments into your resume in all of their soap opera glory and you'll have superhero status in no time and believe me, the CTSO competition judges and employers will take notice.

BRAGGING RIGHTS!

When reading over students applications and resumes, I have noticed a common theme. Students often don't tell their full story and end up leaving the best stuff out. When I have asked students why they inevitably say that it is because they don't want to sound like they are bragging.

Granted, in day-to-day interactions, hearing someone toot their own horn can be a real turn off. On the other hand, the purpose of documenting your accomplishments and sharing your resume is because the reader needs to know what makes you special and different than your competitors. Think of it as branding, not bragging. You have to be your own marketer and PR person. No one knows your story better than you do—so say it loud and say it proud! You are a rock star and you are not afraid for anyone to know it!

ARTIFACTS AND ASSETS

As you prepare for your competition, you will most likely create artifacts to strengthen your presentation or project. In an earlier chapter of your competition journey, you set up a Wakelet account so that you could add all of the awesome ideas for competition readiness to an online collection. Your next step here is to create a new Wakelet collection to keep track of all of your accomplishments. If you get a certificate or you are mentioned by your school on social media or in the news, no matter how small or big, store these accomplishments in your Wakelet collection and refer back to them when it's time to add all of your bragging rights to a resume, portfolio, or even to mention them in an interview. You can keep this collection private so that only you can reference it, or you can create a public collection to use as an online portfolio. The bottom line is, keep track of accomplishments as you go and refer back to them often. Incorporate them into the impression that you give for your written brand.

YOYO
(YOU'RE ON YOUR OWN)

Ask a fellow CTSO member to edit your written materials. Suggest that they start with the last sentence and edit each sentence in reverse, starting at the bottom and working their way back up. This makes it easier to catch mistakes as it is out of context. Be sure to return the favor for them!

Next, proof each other's written materials. Underline the verb, star the noun, and circle any mistakes. This ensures that your sentences are complete and all mistakes are noted and ready to correct. The more eyes on your work, the more opportunities to make it better!

How can you add drama to your resume? Remember, you only get one chance to make a first impression, make your paper impression count!

_____

_____

_____

What are your proudest accomplishments? Now is not the time to be modest, share them loud and proud!

_____

_____

_____

Now add all of this awesomeness to your resume and portfolio!

_____

_____

_____

Speaking of portfolios... use these questions as a guide to creating your Wakelet collection (or another version) of an online, or offline portfolio:

• How will you ensure that artifacts from your competition journey make it to a portfolio?

_____

_____

_____

• What portfolio format will you use?

_____

_____

_____

• What CTSO related experiences will you add to your portfolio?

_____

_____

_____

- What is your biggest motivator for competing? What are your secondary motivators? How are these reflected in your portfolio?

_____

_____

_____

- Ultimately, what do you hope to get out of your CTSO competitions? How is this reflected in your portfolio?

_____

_____

_____

- Who will you need assistance from in creating your portfolio? Are there artifacts that your teachers have on file? Items that your parents/guardians have collected that should be in your portfolio? Do you need to connect with folks from your community to get documentation or pictures of activities and community service events?

_____

_____

_____

Chapter 6

TESTIMONIALS— CAN I GET A WITNESS?

"Great vision without great people is irrelevant."

~ JIM COLLINS

You may be asked to include reference letters or referrals as part of your competition entry requirements. The relationships that you've built over the years will definitely come in handy when tasked with this assignment.

Who should you ask to write references?
Coaches, teachers, counselors, principals, neighbors, pastors, community members, and so on.

Who should not write references?
Aunts, uncles, grandparents, mom, dad, friends, or individuals that you haven't known very long, and certainly not people who (...shockingly!) aren't your biggest fan.

What should you ask them to include?
Make sure that they know what and who the letter is for and give them some talking points on what the judges may be looking for in your reference.

For instance, if you are competing in FFA for horticulture then you may want to include an organizer who oversaw your work and contributions for the community garden. If you are competing in FCCLA for a culinary arts event, tap into the organizers for that soup kitchen that you volunteer at on a regular basis.

Work Ethic, Awards, and Accomplishments
Make sure to provide them with your bio and resume which includes your awards and accomplishments. They need to have enough information so that the reference letter isn't generic and has specific examples to cite—so essentially—you are providing them with a cheat sheet.

How many people should you ask?
Twice as many as you are told that you need. People get busy and tangled up in their own lives, so while someone may have the best intentions to help you out, they just never get to it.

How much time should you give to the person writing on your behalf?
As much as humanly possible, but a minimum of two weeks. Three days before you need it, make sure you very kindly remind him or her by email, phone, or in person.

After the event
Remember to send a thank you card for taking the time to help you and let them know the results! Even if you didn't take home

the gold, you can still be positive and let them know the take aways you were fortunate enough to receive from that experience.

If you are really clever, you can put a tickler on your calendar so that you receive a reminder to send the thank-you cards out after your event. Want to earn even more gold stars? Have the cards or stationary ready to go with an address and stamp on the envelope to make it easier for you to follow through—post competition.

The people who support you now are also the ones who will be around and there for you in the future. This is an important piece of relationship building—not just for now, but for the future you!

> *"Surround yourself with only people who are going to lift you higher. Life is already filled with those who want to bring you down."*
> **~ OPRAY WINFREY**

YOYO
(YOU'RE ON YOUR OWN)

Who knows you best and can speak to your accomplishments? (& **NOT** Mom, Dad, Auntie or your Gramps!)

_____

_____

_____

_____

Use this space to draft your request.

_____

_____

_____

_____

Request Reference Letters ASAP! Send them now!

_____

_____

_____

_____

"Most employers value responsible, hard-working employees who can handle stress, communicate clearly and assertively, act with integrity, find creative solutions to problems, anticipate and manage challenges, resolve conflicts, and get along with coworkers. Every one of these skills is an aspect of emotional intelligence."

~ MAURICE J. ELIAS

Chapter 7

SPOKEN WORD

"The biggest skill people are missing is the ability to communicate: both written and oral presentations. It's a huge problem for us."

~ ANNMARIE NEAL, Vice President for
Talent Management at Cisco Systems

Although each CTSO and competitions within CTSO's require different skill sets, one common denominator between those events with a public speaking component is that presentation skills count and may be the deal breaker between going home with a bronze medal or heading to the next level. This chapter is slightly (slightly may be under-exaggerating) longer than others in this book because it's such an important topic, for competitions AND for life.

In order to excel in any competition (...and in life!), you need to create an interactive and engaging environment that is focused on telling your story. Obviously, you need to reference your scoring rubric to educate your audience, but "edutainment" is what will truly set you apart from the countless competitors who are talking at the judges instead of to the judges.

Think of your best teachers. Are you picturing them? Is he or she lecturing to you or engaging you? No one wants to hear someone drone on and on about a topic, so the trick here is to make the judges feel like they are part of your presentation (...instead of an innocent victim of a presentation that happened to them! Yikes!).

When you are creating, it is crucial that you put yourself in the seat of the audience and determine what would make you really enjoy the story that is unfolding.

THE EYES WIN THE PRIZE

Eye contact is important but sometimes it may be tempting to look more directly at one person when giving the presentation (...perhaps the judge who seems less intimidating!). Regardless, unless you are answering a specific judge directly, it is important to try to give equal eye contact to each judge or audience member so he or she fully believe that you have connected with them.

Have you ever heard the advice that you should find an object behind your audience and talk to it to help relieve nervousness? Or that you should stare at the person's forehead and they won't notice? Forget that you ever heard either piece of well-intended advice, both are terrible ideas and will prevent you from making a real connection with your judges or your audience.

UPTOWN FUNK

Nervous energy takes on many forms. You may suddenly talk more softly or loudly than usual, the pitch of your voice may change, and your body often says more than your words! If you've been told that it appears that you are dancing when giving a presentation, it probably means that rather than pacing, fidgeting, tapping, or other nervous habits—you appear to be dancing.

So take a deep breath, relax, remind yourself that you are simply having a conversation like you have been doing since you learned to talk. Practice videoing yourself to see when your nervous physical behavior begins. What were you thinking of at that point? Was there a question that made you uncomfortable or ill-prepared? Was it when you were struggling with specific wording? Try to identify your triggers and address them. The more prepared you are the less likely your body will act like it has a mind of its' own. Also, be patient and forgiving of yourself. It takes time to break any habit. Just keep practicing, and try not to focus so much on your habit that you lose track of why you are there and what you are attempting to get across to your audience.

Here are some of the common topics compiled from the questions I receive when training students for public speaking.

Winning Your Audience Over... Again!

1. If you notice that people are losing interest, what's the best way to bring them back, even if it wasn't part of the original plan?

   Are you sure they are losing interest? The best way to determine if you have truly lost your audience is to engage with them, if that's an option. Open up the floor for a question or give them an opportunity to engage with one another to discuss the material so far. The best time to tell if they have been listening is when you are no longer talking. If giving the floor to your audience is not an option, find ways to add pizzazz to your presentation by adding variety to your rate of speech, increasing or decreasing body language, or changing your volume.

   The bottom line to ensuring that you are winning over your audience is to be interesting. If you are bored preparing or delivering your talk, your audience will be mind numbed during the delivery.

Tick-Tock

2. How do I stick to the time restrictions?

   It is important to be mindful of time when delivering your presentation. If your presentation runs over the allotted time, you will lose points. Conversely, if you are no longer saying something meaningful and you are simply talking to fill the time, you've said too much. Less is more. If you have a minimum amount of time that you need to speak, be sure to prepare enough meaningful content so that you do not lose points for going under the allotted time. This leads us to the next question...

Prepare, Prepare, Prepare

3. What should you do when you are done presenting and you still have a couple of minutes left?

> *"This is really embarrassing. I was told backstage that I have eighteen minutes. I only prepared fifteen. So if it's cool, I would like to wait for three. I am really sorry."*
>
> **~ ZE FRANK**

Always over prepare. Have additional content that can be added in as to not lose points in your competition for finishing early. Practice and consistently time yourself but know that when you are nervous, the tendency is to speed up. So keep track of your time and have plenty of bonus material that is related. There is no shame in overpreparing!

 TIP:

Here's a handy tool that may help you in getting the timing down, it's a free speech calculator that converts words to minutes: http://www.speechinminutes.com/

---

4. How do I stop stuttering or repeating things like "Ummmm..." when speaking?

    While this can have causes that are due to underlying disease and should be addressed by medical professionals, If this is a problem that you experience only while speaking in public or in a stressful situation, the good news is that you are not alone. Stuttering and using filler words are amongst the most common issue reported in public speaking.

    I can personally relate all too well. In fact, I almost dropped out of my teacher preparation program in college after my professor counted how many times I said, "Ummm" and announced it to the class. I was mortified! Fortunately, I discovered that the more time I spent preparing, the more confident I was when speaking in front of others. I also learned to pause for a moment in place of my go-to filler words and "Ummm".

    While it is true that developers for AI platforms actually include common filler words in their attempts to show how "human" the tech is... the bad news for you is that as a human, who is competing, you will not have the luxury that AI does and you will need to become stronger in this area, especially as you begin to develop your voice. Observing when you are using filler words and practicing the tips that are given throughout this book will help you to improve in this area.

5. How long should pauses be?

    The official answer: it depends! If you are pulling your audience in so that you can reveal something that is jaw-dropping, three full seconds is a good measure. If you are creating wait time so that your audience has time to formulate a response, you may want to give a few additional moments. If you say something humorous, give the audience enough time to enjoy a laugh and to begin to quiet down. As you become more experienced, this will become more natural for you. Until then, practice and ask for feedback on the length of your pauses. Get feedback from multiple people.

    "Great speaking isn't just about words, but about the use of words and what makes a word a word—i.e. the space between words."

    ~ ALF REHN

6. How do I keep from getting distracted while speaking, for instance, if someone walks in the room or leaves?

    Practice speaking with distractions around you. Do you have little brothers and sisters? Practice your speech in the same room where they are playing. If you are practicing with a group of fellow CTSO members, ask them to come in and out of the room while you are practicing. This will help you to develop your focus while presenting.

7. How do you make them pay attention to you?

   Be interesting! Your audience will not be able to keep their attention on your message if you are talking about information that is boring or mundane. Make sure that you are using vivid words that create a mental picture of what you are saying. The tone of your voice and confidence of your delivery also determine if your judges will pay attention to your words. Practice, and get feedback on your delivery. (noticing a theme here?)

8. How do you get your judges pumped up for what you are talking about?

   Emotions are contagious. Your judges will not be any more enthusiastic about what you are talking about than you are. That being said, your judges may need to maintain a professional demeanor and contain their emotional responses to ensure that it doesn't appear as if they are partial or giving too much away during the judging process. Don't take this personally. Do your best!

9. I am signing up for a team event, but my partner is shy. What is the best and nicest way to "push" my teammate into speaking during our event?

   Start practicing together as early as possible and during this time, help your teammate to get out of their comfort zone. Arrange practices in front of different audiences so that your teammate becomes accustomed to getting out of their comfort zone. Give your teammate lots of positive feedback.

Focus on what they are doing well and help to build up their speaking prowess by showing them how valuable their words are. You may be giving them a gift by helping them to share their ideas and giving strength to their words.

10. How do I keep my voice from shaking when I am speaking in front of the judges or an audience?

A shaky voice is a natural response to a stressful situation. Speaking in public is a stressful situation! Your fight or flight responses kick in and can cause your body to do unusual things. Try this: try to get your voice to shake like that when you aren't nervous. Or your knees to shake... or your hands to tremble... It's quite impressive really. Embrace and accept that you are human AND you are alive! Also, acknowledge that what you are feeling is a natural response. Take a deep breath. Remember that your judges and/or your audience want you to be successful. Relax and embrace this moment that you have spent so much time preparing for. The more you get out of your comfort zone and push through the shakiness, the easier it gets. Keep putting yourself out there, even after the competition is over. You've got this!

Also, don't give your attention to your voice when it shakes. Instead, speak a little louder. Tighten your diaphragm. Notice what happens... usually within a minute or two, the shakiness subsides and is replaced by your strong, confident self. In addition, your audience doesn't notice the shakiness as much as you do. Don't get hung up on this.

11. What should I do to feel more comfortable speaking in front of the judges?

Practice speaking in front of strangers. Practice your talk in front of multiple audiences—friends, families, classmates, during CTSO meetings, on a Google Hangout with someone on a different part of the globe. It takes practice to feel comfortable. Most likely you will still feel some nervous energy, but you will be confident that you know what you are talking about and how to say it. Watch Amy Cuddy's TED Talk on youtube and learn how to "Fake it until you become it" through power posing. Also, read work through this companion guide in its entirety, work through all of the exercises, and you will feel much, much, much more confident and comfortable speaking in front of your judges.

12. Will I ever truly master public speaking?

Yes and no. Yes, you will improve tremendously and you will feel more and more confident over time. No, you will never master public speaking in the sense that you've arrived and you are done mastering this skill. Like most things in life, there's always room to continue to improve and to learn new tricks and techniques. Embrace this, and enjoy the journey!

13. How do I improve my diction?

Some sources suggest practicing tongue twisters to improve diction and clarity of speech. Tongue twisters do not seem to work for all people though, for instance, me! Tongue twisters just trip me up. Period. And they do not replicate an authentic experience. I recommend reading difficult passages aloud and focusing on over-exaggerating as you enunciate each word, even simple words like "and" or "the". This helps you to become cognizant of the pacing and the feel of the word in its full glory. When speaking in day-to-day conversations, be aware of your diction. If you develop good habits in all of your conversations, it will show when speaking to your judges or on a stage.

14. When I am stuck and don't know what to say, what do I do?

Have talking points planned that are related to your topic. When someone is getting ready for a media interview, they prepare by coming up with three talking points that they feel are most important to get across. Once you have your three talking points, come up with three ways to say each of your talking points. Congratulations, you now have nine statements that you can connect to what your judges are asking. Try to find bridges between the question and your main ideas that you are an expert on.

INC recommends sticking to your talking points "by redirecting the conversation using 'bridging statements' such as:

- 'I think the question we really ought to ask is...'
- 'That's not my area of expertise, but what I can tell you is...'
- 'Let me put it in perspective.'"

Okay... the first bullet may work in situations outside of responding to your judges, but we will leave it here for other conversations!

15. What do you do if you make a weird sound while talking?

Keep going and do not bring attention to the sound that you made. Most likely, your audience didn't notice or will forget about the noise if you do not draw attention to it. If it's obvious that your judges heard the weird noise, simply say, "excuse me" and keep going where you left off.

16. How do I keep from using the wrong words?

Learn everything about the topic that you can. Memorize and practice using vocabulary associated with the topic. The more you know your subject, the more confident you will be, and you will be less likely to forget your words.

17. What is a good speaking tempo?

For most cases, go for a goldilocks tempo—not too fast and not too slow. Speaking faster and louder does add auditory interest in some cases, as does speaking softer and slower, but again, use these for emphasis and to add variety. Stick to your goldilocks tempo for 80% of your talk.

18. How long should the introduction be?

Only as long as it needs to be. Make sure you've given some background information, and then dive into the main course.

19. How do you keep the judges' attention if the presentation has difficulties?

Try to prevent difficulties from occurring in the first place. Plan for every worst-case scenario. Visualize every aspect of your presentation and anticipate every possible need. If difficulties do happen, think on your toes and resolve them as quickly as possible. Be prepared to improvise. Talk to your judges and make small talk as you work to recover from the difficulties.

20. I talk fast. How do I pace myself?

Practice in front of a mirror and say your speech dramatically slow. Draw out every word. It may feel and sound silly at first, but it will help you to slow down when you talk in front of your judges. Next, download the Teleprompter Lite app. This app allows you to paste your script and then play it as your record yourself reading the lines out loud. The script scrolls up, just like a teleprompter, except you are able to see yourself behind the words. You have the option to slow down the speed of the teleprompter feed by moving the pace towards the turtle. For faster speeds, you move the speed towards the rabbit. For now, focus on creating an unnaturally slow speed to get used to breathing between words and slowing down your pace. When you are speaking in front of the judges or an audience, remind yourself of how your breathing feels when you are slowing down your pace. Incorporate that breathing into your talk. Keep practicing this until it feels natural to speak more slowly in front of judges.

When in doubt, take a moment to pause and breathe.

21. How do I keep the judges engaged?

Be engaging! As the presenter, you set the tone and the level of enthusiasm. Make that connection and make sure your energy is contagious!

22. What if there are more judges than I expected and I don't have enough materials for everyone?

Bring more copies and materials than you think you will need. Always over prepare. If you still do not have enough, try to find a way to make light of the shortage. Simply ask them to share. If it feels natural to do so, make a comment indicating that you are trying to be kind to the environment by using fewer materials or finding ways to conserve the budget at your school.

Also, don't get too hung up over things that you cannot change. Focus on what is in your circle of control at that moment. In this instance, it is too late to do anything about the number of supplies, so be graceful, your judges will understand, and focus on being amazing!

23. How do I respond to awkward questions from the judges?

Most likely, the question just seems awkward at the moment. Politely ask your judge if they can rephrase the question. You may also want to consider restating the question out loud and asking the judge if you have understood them correctly. For example, if the judge gives you the following prompt:

"There are defects throughout an entire order. It's due for delivery tomorrow. What do you think we should do?"

As a competitor, you may want to get clarity on your role and restate the question in the following manner:

"In this scenario, I am playing the role of a manager and am tasked with making a decision regarding how to handle a mishap that has caused defects throughout an order. I need to decide next steps as this is a time sensitive matter and customers are counting on my team. Is that correct?"

By restating the question and getting clarity, you've also given yourself time to process the question and potential solutions. Practice restating questions in a pleasant manner prior to competitions in which judges will be asking you questions, such as interviews and impromptu events.

24. How do I keep from being nervous when speaking to the judges?

Assume positive intentions. Your judges are volunteering their time to be there, and they want you to be successful! Take a deep breath as you are walking into your event. Smile. Relax your shoulders. Have a positive mantra that you repeat to yourself to help shape your positive self-talk. Visit chapter 13 for more on getting to know who your judges are and how to connect with your judges rather than feeling intimidated by them.

25. How do I stay mindful of the rules of presenting while presenting?

Practice the rules of presenting until they become a habit. Ultimately, you want the rules of presenting to become so ingrained that it appears as if it just comes naturally. Remember, it takes a ton of practice to appear natural when it comes to public speaking.

26. How do I get good at speaking with little preparation?

Great question. You don't. Refer to the question above, number 25. To add to this, folks who are invited to deliver a TED Talk on the main TED stage have sometimes practiced their talk over 200 times. Most have spent the six months prior to their talk practicing for that one 18 minute presentation. As a professional speaker, I typically spend 90+ hours preparing a new presentation. This includes research, creating visuals, and practicing the talk. That's two forty hour work weeks for one talk! I don't always have time to put that much preparation into a talk, so if the preparation time is short, I make sure that I am talking about something that I am well versed in and feel comfortable discussing.

Even improv requires preparation. Do a Google search for the rules of improvisation and you will learn how to think through your improv scenario, how to interact with your team during the improv, and how to connect concepts that you have already developed.

27. How can I be inspirational?

If you are competing in an event that has a component that allows you to be inspirational, tell a story that is a first-hand experience. This could be connected to your CTSO journey or another situation that has had a significant impact and that had a lesson to be learned that is transferable.

If sharing a personal story, test it on a trusted teacher, friend, or family member for feedback to ensure that it is at an appropriate level and doesn't contain material that is too sensitive in nature to share with judges who you are meeting for the first time. Also, if it is emotionally charged, make sure it is something that you have dealt with and that you are comfortable sharing.

Once you have identified your story and content, give it your all! In order to be inspirational, you must deliver your story in an inspired manner. Show your passion. Don't hold back!

28. I don't know what to do with my hands or body.

Visit chapter 8 for the full scoop on body language, but for now, be natural! If in doubt, keep your hands hanging loosely to your side and then use your hands to emphasize your words, as appropriate. Avoid closing your arms, clasping your hands, or doing anything that makes you appear to be closed off. Otherwise, it is really up to you to decide how much or how little you use your hands and body movement. Some speakers are naturally animated with body movements.

Others, like Adam Grant, have limited body movement and hand gestures, but instead use voice variety, facial expressions and eye contact that says it all. The bottom line is to have a message that matters and say it in a way that drives home your idea.

29. How do I properly express my message?

There's more than one right way to deliver your message. Practice sharing your message in different ways and in front of different audiences. Remember, an audience can be one person, many people, or even recording your message on a device to share and get feedback from others. Get feedback on what resonates with your audience. Ultimately, decide on which delivery feels right to you—from the words themselves to body language, to pacing.

30. How do I stand when speaking to the judges?

Standing in front of your judges may seem awkward, especially if you are standing and your judges are sitting and filling out score sheets based on your performance. Focus on your message, not on how awkward the situation feels. Remember why you are there and what you need to communicate to the judges. Try not to fidget or shift your weight, simply stand with feet shoulder-width apart. Pull your shoulders back and away from your ears. Try to find a balance between feeling relaxed and looking natural.

31. How do I give a speech without talking too fast?

Talk slower. Practice talking slower prior to your event. Practice breathing as you speak and taking a moment to pause when you feel yourself speeding up your rate of speech.

32. How do I balance etiquette with passion and drive?

It's not a zero-sum game—there's not an either or in competitions.

According to Wikipedia, "Etiquette is a code of behavior that delineates expectations for social behavior according to contemporary conventional norms within a society, social class, or group." When expressing your passion and drive for your content, do not deviate from societal norms and a professional code of behavior.

33. How do I recover if I lose my way and forget what comes next?

It is not uncommon to forget your words or lose track of where you are in a talk when the pressure is up and the stakes are high. Try pausing for a moment and taking a deep breath. Your judges or audience will not notice the break in most cases, or may even think that you have added space to emphasize a point. Usually, that moment will be enough to regain your thoughts and recapturing your words. If you are able to use notes, keep a "confidence card" in a pocket. A confidence card has keywords that are in order that serves as an outline for your talk. Do not put full sentences or your entire talk as it will be hard to find your place. Just knowing that you have your confidence card, aka cheat sheet, sometimes gives you the confidence to not even need to reference it. If neither of these work, simply skip ahead to the next piece that you remember.

34. How do I speak with flow?

The more you have practiced your talk and the more familiar you are with your topic, the more natural your talk will feel and will flow naturally. Learn all that you can about your topic so that you've truly mastered it. Your speech will be more fluid as a result.

35. What does lectern etiquette mean?

A lectern is a stand on the stage that is used to hold the notes, laptop, or other materials for the individual who is speaking. To remember this word, think, "Lectures are given behind lecterns." A lectern is frequently called a podium, which is inaccurate. A podium is a small stool behind the lectern that is used to give a speaker a taller appearance or to help an individual to be able to see over the lectern into the crowd.

Lectern etiquette is the proper rules to follow when speaking behind a lectern, such as do not touch the lectern, stand 3-4 inches away from the lectern, do not lean into the microphone when speaking from behind a lectern, and use exaggerated facial expressions since your body language is hidden.

36. Will the judges look at my social media?

Probably not. That being said, if you are concerned, there's no better time than now to start deliberately curating your online brand.

37. How do I deal with stage fright?

First, change the words that you use and your mental self-talk. Instead of fright, think of what you are feeling as excitement. Have you ever been on a rollercoaster ride? Remember the feelings in your stomach, the racing pulse, the energy... prior to getting on the ride? Or being strapped in and the ride is about to take off and you have so much excitement pumping through your veins? The same fight or flight response that creates the excitement that you feel before riding a roller coaster is the energy you are feeling before you speak in public. Changing your words from fright to excitement will give a positive spin that enhances your talk and gives it oomph.

38. How do I tailor my myself towards my judges?

When preparing for the spoken portion of your presentation, keep your audience in mind. Make sure you have a professional tone and that your word choice is geared towards an audience that is older than you, not towards peers. Have a professional appearance and feel to your talk.

39. How do I make my speech powerful?

Talk about something that matters and makes an impact. Use powerful words, a strong voice, and bold body language. Make sure that you are talking about a powerful topic.

40. I would like to learn how to speak without a script. Where do I start?

Start with a script and practice a few times with reading the words. As you become more comfortable with the content, switch to practicing your talk with just an outline. From there, move to practicing with just keywords on a notecard. Before you know it, you will be able to deliver your talk without a script.

If you wish to memorize your talk word for word, create strong images to attach to the keywords. Print out a copy of the script in double or triple space. Draw images above the keywords or concepts so that you can begin to create a mental picture of your talk. Visualize these images as you are practicing and this will help you to memorize your talk.

41. What do I do if I mispronounce a name in an important setting?

Say the correct name, and keep going. You can also say, Excuse me, and then the correct pronunciation. Try not to say "sorry" or "I apologize" as this can weaken your message in this setting. Also, avoid giggling or adding extra commentary that draws more attention to the mistake.

42. Where do I put my hands when speaking?

Start with your hands to your side. As you begin speaking, add in hand gestures and body language that feels natural and not forced. Stay tuned for the next chapter which will dig into the subject of body language in more detail!

Advice from your peers who have gone before you. When asked, "What is the best piece of advice that you have for CTSO members who are working on improving their public speaking and presence during the verbal portion of a competition?" Here are some of the top pieces of advice from fellow CTSO competitors:

1) Practice a lot! Make eye contact and use your hands to talk!
2) Fake it until you make it.
3) Manifest good vibes.
4) Don't underestimate yourself.
5) Always try to make eye contact.
6) For public speaking, there are many methods which may help you to improve on all areas; projection, nerves, memorization, etc. Methods like power posing before speaking, recording yourself presenting the speech and analyzing where to improve.
7) Don't overthink, focus on your goal.
8) Run, sprint, exercise. Get your blood flowing the morning of a competition, it's so important to allow your mind to connect with your body and to center yourself physically. You'll be able to carry that energy with you on stage.

9) Focus on the message and what you want to say rather than the thought of people seeing you negatively.

10) Be a speaker that you would want to listen to, someone that would capture your attention.

11) Practice in front of their family members first. It is embarrassing but they'll soon realize that it is by far one of the better choices that they got. If not that, to choose someone they trust wholeheartedly and speak in front of them. Also to be able to take constructive criticism when given.

12) Don't be nervous about it because it gets easier as you continue your speech.

13) Practice in front of a mirror. Don't wing it at the event.

14) I recommend practicing with peers or your parents.

15) Stay cool, calm and collected. Speak slowly and clearly.

"One quick tip that I would suggest is recording your voice reading the speech as if you were performing it. Knowing HOW you want to say your speech will improve the memorization aspect of training before a competitive event. I personally recorded my speech for my state officer campaign and I was able to memorize the content of the speech and the delivery of my speech effectively."

~ JAIME PEREZ, State Officer

16) Step outside of your comfort zone and have fun with it.

17) Prepare meetings in school and practice presenting in front of their teammates.

18) Worrying about it will make you stutter or mess up, try focusing on someone or something.
19) Keep calm, breathe in for four seconds and out for eight seconds. Clear your mind.
20) Try practicing in front of your mirror, friends and family members, that way you will be less flustered when speaking in front of a large group of people.
21) Just be confident in what you say.
22) Practice in front of people you know, like friends, then it will be easier to be able to present to strangers.
23) Practice in front of trusted friends, family, or in front of a mirror. Always project so everyone can hear clearly
24) Have eye contact, be confident, practice.
25) Try practicing on a smaller audience first.
26) Try practicing with someone or use a mirror.
27) Perform in front of a mirror or someone you are comfortable with to boost your confidence
28) Learn from an expert.
29) Make eye contact and be confident. Speak with passion.
30) Relax, pace yourself as you speak, do not speak too fast where no one can understand you. Just practice the material and have note cards with points on it to remind you of what you are talking about.
31) Be yourself. If you change who you are when you're speaking, you are not representing your character. When it comes down to presenting, be you!
32) Relax. Just think about you are talking to your friend or even play your favorite song and jam out to relax and dance your stress out.

33) Confidence is key when it comes to public speaking. If you're not absolutely positive about what you're speaking about, it will not turn out good! The audience can always tell if you know what you're talking about or not.

34) Just keep trying, don't be afraid to go outside of your comfort zone.

35) Just breathe and it's ok to take breaks to gather your thoughts.

36) Practice a lot and stay focused on what you are saying.

37) Practice your vocabulary and make sure you are speaking properly.

38) The biggest components that student forget when speaking are taking their time, breathing, and making eye contact. Simple breathing exercises can make all the difference between a speech the is enjoyable to listen to and one that is rushed and tense.

39) Take your time, make direct eye contact, and don't say um or like.

40) Always pronounce your words, don't mumble.

41) It gets easier to talk to a group of people over time.

42) When speaking, make sure you are talking loud enough for everyone to hear and look at your audience.

43) Find people in the crowd that you know.

44) Talk about something that you feel confident about.

45) The best advice I can give is treating it as if you were speaking to a relative or friend. I can feel intimidated by others I do not know, so I always try to make sure to practice with friends and family, then present to others I may not be entirely comfortable with.

46) Every time you lose your train of thought rather than saying um taking a pause and think about what you are going to say next.

47) The more you work on improving the better and easier it would be for you to do/be a part of the competition.

48) Keep your hands out of your pockets.

49) Make sure you memorize or at least have some other way of remembering anything just so you have the points that you'll be presenting.

50) One strategy I learned from people that do voice acting Is to record your lines then play them aloud. Listen to how you sound. Memorize it. Improve upon It. You'll do just fine.

51) Don't overthink what you've prepared and be confident in yourself that you know the information. And whatever you do, don't let the audience know you messed up because at the end of the day you're the only one who knows what was prepared.

"If you can't communicate and talk to other people and get across your ideas, you're giving up your potential."

~ WARREN BUFFETT

GUEST VOICE: SAM BHAT
Law Student at Brooklyn Law School
JD 2022

Advice for Public Speaking

Public speaking can be a terrifying challenge, no matter your age or experience. We've been taught to think about oral presentation as being somehow different from our natural ability to share ideas and communicate with each other. Think about it: we answer questions, make decisions, and communicate our thoughts with little preparation every day. But even though we use our voice every day, it seems to escape us when it's time to give a speech.

This is in part to blame for feelings of nervousness or anxiety. When we are feeling put "on the spot", our body's parasympathetic nervous system kicks in: we sweat, fidget, and feel butterflies in our stomach. Our body's internal animal instinct says "This is dangerous, get me out!" Understanding that this is what is taking place is the first step to overcoming it. Breathe deeply, to the bottom of your stomach. When we are anxious, our breaths become shallow and we hold air in our upper lungs, causing tension in our chest and neck. By breathing deep, we are reassuring our body that we are safe and not in danger. When we do this, we remember that we have been practicing and know what we are doing. This will help us focus on what we want to say.

In many competitions, we can prepare for the event ahead of time. Even in those events for which we receive the performance prompt at the time of competition, we can simulate our events and use older prompts from previous competitions to practice with. Getting a feel for what it will look and feel like on the day of competition is very important, and there are a few things you can do to prepare. With each of the steps below, we are practicing the process of competition, so that it will not feel alien to us at the time of our event:

1. Ask teachers or professionals in your community to "judge" you. Provide them with practice prompts and rubrics, and simulate the timed conditions of your event. Your adviser will have access to these materials, and you can also find them online. These materials are invaluable in the preparation process.

2. Remember that it is your presentation. If you are using prepared notes, be comfortable with the material so that you are **not reading** from your material. Be confident in what you are saying, and use your practice time to develop a delivery strategy. If you do not have prepared notes and will be receiving your prompt at the event, create an outline for how you can answer any case, and commit that outline to memory. By the time if your event, neither your prepared notes nor a new prompt should look unfamiliar, and there will be no reason to panic.

3. Practice maintaining good eye contact. Confidence translates to how we say things, and as the saying goes "What we say is not as important as how we say it." When we speak to our friends, eye contact occurs as a natural component of nonverbal communication. When we are consciously thinking about it however, it can be difficult to make eye contact as we feel shy, or even scared. If we are using prepared notes, it can be helpful to make line breaks in our notes— reminding us to look up. If we are speaking from memory or extemporaneously, it is helpful to practice speaking to the judge, remembering that we are simply having a conversation and conveying

information. Making this as natural as possible during practice will go a long way to ensuring that on game day, we walk into our competition with a smile on our face, ready to greet the judge.

With practice comes confidence. Simulating the conditions of your event in the single most important thing you can do for yourself ahead of your competition. There shouldn't be any surprises on the day of your event, and you can make sure that will be the case by paying attention to detail and delivery during your preparation. If you practice, nothing will happen on the day of your event that you haven't already encountered, and you'll be ready to perform to the best of your ability. Take a deep breath and let it fly—you're ready for this.

YOYO
(YOU'RE ON YOUR OWN)

What are your strengths when it comes to public speaking? List them below and then find ways to capitalize on what you know you are already doing well.

_____

_____

_____

_____

What are three areas of refinement that you would like to focus on improving? Even the most seasoned public speakers are constantly looking for ways to improve. Try to pick only a few at a time to work on as it can be overwhelming if you are trying to do too much.

_____

_____

_____

_____

Find a trusted individual to watch you speak and provide you with feedback. Tell them exactly what you want feedback on—this shouldn't be a free for all for them to provide input on every aspect of your performance. Ask them what to look for. If you are working on eliminating filler words, ask them to count how many times you say um or so. Or ask them if there are gaps in your presentation where you need to provide more information. Whatever the area, make sure you take the feedback as a gift to help improve and do not look at it as a weakness.

_____

_____

_____

_____

"Don't measure anything unless the data helps you make a better decision or change your actions. If you're not prepared to change your diet or your workouts, don't get on the scale."

~ SETH GODIN

Chapter 8

YOUR BODY—THE TATTLE-TAIL!

Nonverbal cues often say more than the words that competitors use. Whether it's your posture, hand gestures, body movement, eye contact, or facial expressions, each plays a huge role in the delivery of your presentation.

Keep the following in mind while preparing and practicing the spoken portion of your presentation:

DO

Move It Like You Mean It

Include meaningful movements when you are competing. If you are delivering a speech without a podium and you are speaking to more than a handful of people, move with purpose, take a few steps in the direction of the people sitting furthest away in order to make better eye contact and ensure that they feel included. Don't forget the other side of the room though! After a few moments or a few sentences, take a step or two in another direction to address another part of your audience. This will also help to prevent awkwardness, fidgeting or shifting your weight.

The Ten-Mile Smile

Smiling is contagious. When you smile, the instinct is for someone to smile back at you. Smiling activates neural messaging that benefits your health and happiness because the feel-good neurotransmitters called dopamine, endorphins and serotonin—are all released the moment a smile flashes across your face.

Why does this matter? By now, we are all on the same page about how intimidating judges can be—right? By smiling, you look and feel like you are having a great time and even the scariest judge will instantly feel like they are having a good time too! And let's face it, do you want Simon Cowell or Paula Abdul when you are singing your song (...or in this case—delivering your presentation.). The happy judge votes happy. So smile. Big time.

Breathe

In. Out. Repeat.

Why? Well first and foremost, it is a human requirement to continue living... but then I bet you already knew that. Obviously, air flow means you are still speaking to your audience, but the more you can control your breath, the more you can control the rest of your delivery. Prior to your presentation, begin to practice eight-count breaths until it is so natural, you don't have to think about it at all.

Another great trick, is to yawn as big and as long as you can (...but make sure this is BEFORE you are in front of the judges!). Yawning is an excellent way to loosen your body and breathe deeply while loosening your jaw, which may have a tendency to tense under pressure.

DON'T

Crossed = Closed

Don't close off your body with your arms. Stay open and receptive. Mirror what you want to see in your judges. A judge with crossed arms stopped listening a long time ago. By opening your own body language and delivering your message, the judges will naturally be wooed into doing the same.

Fidgit, Shift, Panic

Avoid shifting your weight or fidgeting. Both of these are the dreaded telltale signs that you are nervous and this behavior will distract your listeners from the message that you intend to deliver.

YOYO
(YOU'RE ON YOUR OWN)

Now it's time to practice your body language.

Find a friend. Ask them to time you for two minutes while you share a portion of your presentation. Start with your arms by your side. As it feels natural to do so, use your hands and body to emphasize what you are saying. Get feedback from your friend on how natural it appeared. Jot down notes here for what you are doing well, and areas to continue to practice on.

_____

_____

_____

_____

Go to YouTube and watch TED Talks, political debates, and interviews. But here's the caviat—watch them on silent. What does the body language give away about the person's confidence, their perceived competency level, or how likable they are? Record your thoughts below and include what areas caused individuals to appear closed off, aka, what not replicate in your own public speaking style.

_____

_____

_____

_____

Practice your talk in the mirror. What body language enhances your message? Add more of what works while minimizing anything that detracts from your message.

_____

_____

_____

_____

Chapter 9

MASTERING THE IMPROMPTU COMPETITIVE EVENT

Impromptu speaking takes on many forms—Interviewing and Role-Play are two common forms that are common in CTSO events

I was at a CTSO state conference recently and was facilitating a preparation room for students to stop in and get feedback from their practice time for the competition. I saw a few students hanging out in the hallway and invited them in. They explained that they couldn't prepare for the competition and had to "wing it" as they were doing role plays.

C'mon. Really? Is anyone buying that? There's plenty to do to prepare for a role play... like... hmmm—practicing role plays?

TIPS FOR MASTERING ROLE-PLAY EVENTS

1. Once you know the category, brainstorm all of the potential role plays that you can come up with.
2. See if you can find out what past role-plays have been within your category and practice those scenarios.
3. When you are ready to compete in the role-play, read it carefully and then reread it again... even more carefully. Make sure you fully understand the prompt and whatever you do—do not rush the preparation piece.
4. Decide what the judges will be looking for in your delivery. What is the prompt asking? What role will you be playing?

Preparation is key in competition, as well as every other aspect of life, and this habit—is one that is truly worthy of being picked up.

INTERVIEW LIKE A PRO!

Most CTSO's have a competitive event that is dedicated to interviewing skills. Being able to perform well under the stress of an interview is a life skill that will serve you well in both formal and informal situations where you will need to sell yourself to a potential employer, or sell a product to a future client.

On a personal note, it wasn't until 15 years into my career that I actually had the opportunity to practice interview skills. During a leadership class, while working on my Master's degree in Educational Leadership, we had a surprise component—superintendents, principals, and other education leaders had been invited to interview each of us and provide feedback on our interview skills. I found the process to be extremely valuable and wished that I had had this opportunity years earlier. Congratulations, your competitive event is granting you this opportunity!

Prior to the interview simulation, you will submit documents such as a resume, cover letter, portfolio, reference letters, or other documentation that the judges will request to review. Be sure to review chapters 6 and 7 on Written Word and Spoken Word to help prepare for your event.

As a CTSO judge, I remember a particular incident in which the competitor seemed completely unprepared. When the interview question, "How did you prepare for this interview" came up, the student said that she was sitting outside waiting for her turn and asked a friend who was waiting for her for some tips... That was it... nothing more. As you might suspect, this individual's entry went to the bottom of the stack.

DO take the time to prepare for the interview! Many of the tips found throughout this book apply here, such as resume tips, spoken word, how to handle pre-competition jitters, dressing for success, and more. Be sure to read this book in its entirety to ensure that you are ready for the interview competitive event and, more importantly, real-world interviews.

Prepare anecdotes in advance. (Remember? You are a storyteller!) For example, perhaps you can prepare your anecdote by expanding on a few of these responses:

What is your greatest weakness?
Describe your history in this area.

Tell me about a time that you put someone else's needs ahead of your own.

How do you handle pressure?

Where do you plan to be in ten years?

Who inspired you to get where you are today?

YOYO
(YOU'RE ON YOUR OWN)

Do a Google search for basic improv techniques. Which of the techniques are ones that you want to practice incorporating into your style?

_____

_____

_____

_____

Visit the CTSO Competition Readiness Guide Companion Wakelet Collection Link: https://wke.lt/w/s/K7rYXN. Locate the item entitled, "Improv One-Minute Talks." Follow the instructions on this card to practice being able to quickly connect ideas to images, thus improving your Impromptu prowess. After a few rounds, use the space below to reflect on the process.

_____

_____

_____

_____

Schedule practice interviews. Get used to responding to interview questions and improvising on questions that you didn't expect. After the practice interview, go back and review the questions and re-think your responses. How can you

Ace the interview with these counter-intuitive tips: https://www.entrepreneur.com/article/301173

Chapter 10

THE ELEVATOR PITCH

Regardless of the event that you are competing in, an elevator pitch is a must! It can sometimes provide material for your impromptu talks as well! An elevator pitch is a brief, persuasive speech that you can use to spark a decision maker's interest and should last no longer than the time it would take to ride in an elevator. This term originated back in the studio days of Hollywood, when a screenwriter would catch (...some may even say stalk!) an unsuspecting executive on an elevator ride—and pitch him or her the big idea—but they only had so many floors to get the message out and capture the interest of their captive audience.

This skill is tremendously important for you to learn (even if you aren't making a movie!). One scenario that you may have to face is that a judge may ask you to explain what it is that you do, why you do it, how you do it, and why it matters. Could you answer those questions today? If you said no, how and when will you begin preparing for that line of questioning?

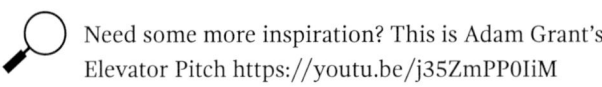 Need some more inspiration? This is Adam Grant's CTSO Elevator Pitch https://youtu.be/j35ZmPP0IiM

Elevator pitches can take many forms. Being able to give a description of your organization in as few as 12 words is sometimes recommended. It's short enough to make an impact and cause the listener to want to know more and ask questions but long enough to get your primary premise across to your audience.

As a reminder, this is just a framework. You will then need to adjust this pitch to meet the needs of your audience. In this circumstance, the audience is the judge. Is your judge evaluating a group competition? You may want to tailor your message to emphasize the importance of developing the skill of teamwork and how your competition has allowed you to grow in this area.

YOYO
(YOU'RE ON YOUR OWN)

Journal It

Use these posts to help create your elevator pitch.

https://plus.google.com/101811969346301599051/posts/cTB2YvXpoyn
http://www.teachliketed.org/2017/05/ElevatorSpeech.html

Read your elevator out loud or even to a friend or family member. Does it sound natural? If not, adjust accordingly.

_____

_____

_____

How will your elevator pitch be different if speaking to an advisor from another school versus a judge who is from a specific business or industry? How will you adjust it if talking to a student who is a year younger and explaining why they should get involved with your CTSO next year? Practicing adjusting your pitch will help you to be able to make your elevator pitch a natural part of a response or conversation.

_____

_____

_____

Chapter 11

DEMONSTRATIONS IN COMPETITIVE EVENTS

"Demos are much more difficult than presentations because, in a demonstration, you must simultaneously focus on the customer, the effect the demonstration is having on the customer, and the mechanics of the demonstration. So it's utter madness to try to give a demonstration without rehearsing it at least three times."

~ GEOFFREY JAMES, Author, and Speaker

Many events require a hands-on demonstration of the skills related to your competition. Once you know what your demonstration will be, write out a step-by-step outline of your demonstration and include what you will say, if there's a verbal component, what you will be doing each step of the way, and what supplies you will need for each step and a break down of how much time is needed for each segment. Even if this is not a requirement for you to turn into anyone for your event, you should do it anyway, as it will help you to organize your thoughts and help you be prepared to practice your demonstration. During the process of writing everything out, you may also identify glitches that need to be worked out before you begin practicing your demonstration.

Professionalism goes beyond appearance, show your professionalism in your demo as well—use technical terms but explain what they mean as you go so that the judge knows that you understand what you are talking about.

In the Inc.com article, *"Give a Great Product Demo: 5 Rules"*, Geoffrey James shares tips on how to turn a step-by-step demo into a story (...do you see how this storytelling thing keeps coming up? I wasn't kidding!). Delivering your demo in the form of a story is a great way to make your demonstration stand out and allows the judges to see the application of what is occurring.

 Source: https://www.inc.com/geoffrey-james/give-a-great-product-demo-5-rules.html

Some demonstrations do not allow for verbal communication during the competition and may be simply be demonstrating while judges are watching and making notes on a clipboard. So pay attention to the details... your judges will be! Safety and sanitation, for instance, apply in multiple CTSO events. Although you may not be verbally communicating your understanding of what the guidelines are, be sure to be very transparent and cognizant of following the rules. Your judges will be noting any violations or perceived violations, so don't slip up on this.

MOCK DEMONSTRATIONS

It is important for you to have practiced your demonstration multiple times in front of different audiences to ensure that you feel confident in front of the judges and you are used to performing in front of strangers.

You may also want to request to do the demo in front of your class in order to get feedback from your peers who know your content area and may catch details that need extra attention.

Once you have the opportunity to practice in front of people you know, request to do your demo in front of others who will be more objective. Most advisors have business and industry connections who may be willing to do a mock competition and give you feedback on your demonstration. The key to this is having the courage to ask. Know that most people are in your corner and want you to succeed and the worst thing that can happen is that he or she will not have time and then you simply move on to your next choice.

HOW WILL FEEDBACK BE GIVEN?

Do you want your mock judges to give you written feedback? Verbal feedback? Both? Decide how you will receive the information in a way that best informs your presentation and let those who are helping you know your preference ahead of time.

Also, make sure that you have copies of the rubric for your mock judges to use during your demonstration.

BEFORE LEAVING TO GO YOUR COMPETITION

The Big Bin

Double check your list of materials to ensure that you have everything. As an FCCLA advisor, my students had bins with all of their materials and checklist of everything that they needed in a sheet protector taped to the top of the bin. The students had their bins ready a few days before the event. One time, when we arrived at the competition and students were beginning the cooking demo, one of the students discovered that some of the items that she needed were missing. She later found out from another student that someone in an evening class needed materials for a lab with another instructor and "borrowed" the items from her bin but never returned them. So err on the side of being over prepared on the day of your competition as well and check your supplies again before leaving and one final time prior to your presentation.

Close Your Eyes and Visualize

Visualize yourself going through each step of the demonstration. What are you doing? What are you saying? Picture yourself in all of your full-color glory, pulling off a flawless performance and doing your best demo yet. Mentally walking through each step is a technique that is used by athletes, performers, and even surgeons and there is even evidence that your brain doesn't know the difference between the visualization and the actual event.

FINAL TIPS AND REMINDERS

1. Don't wait until the last minute to arrange for your mock demos and invite mock judges. Plan early.
2. Give the mock judges copies of the competition guidelines and scoring criteria prior to the mock event so that they have an opportunity to review the expectations and are able to give you quality feedback.
3. Arrange for more mock demos than you think you will need as it is possible that one or two could be canceled due to last minute conflicts.
4. Determine if your mock judges will be coming to your school or another location
5. Have a list and check it twice! Make sure you have all of your materials and label your bin accordingly.
6. Make sure you have a memorable closing for your demo as the opening and closing is what lingers in the mind of your judges and audience.
7. Give a sincere thanks to your judges.
8. When appropriate, shake hands with each judge, make eye contact, and thank them individually.

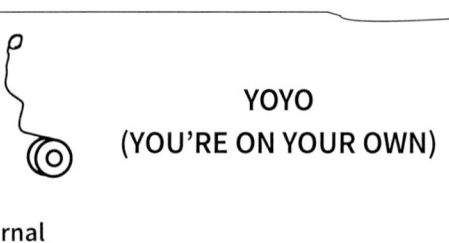

YOYO
(YOU'RE ON YOUR OWN)

Journal

What is your timeline for getting your mock demonstrations done prior to your competitive event?

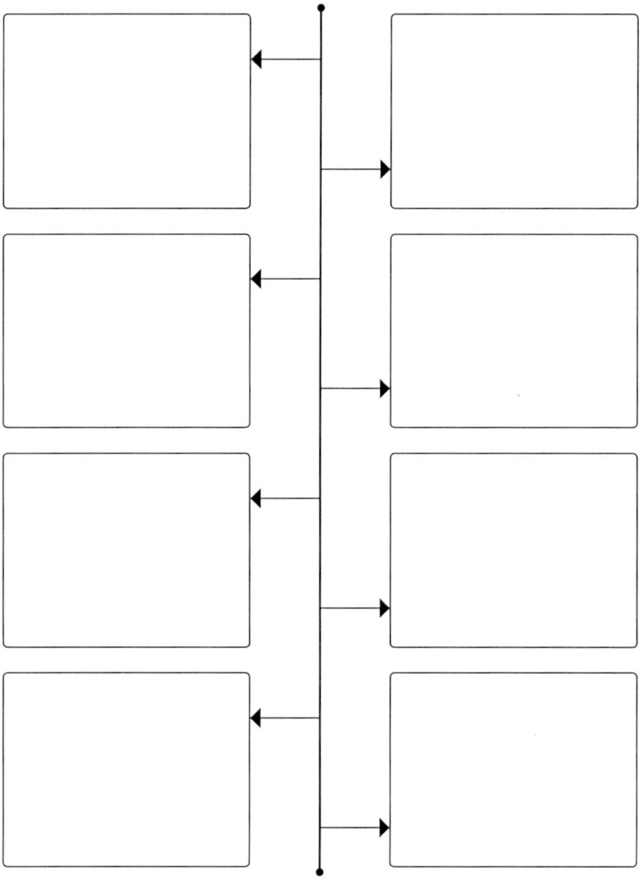

Brainstorm all of the potential individuals who may be able to serve as mock judges.

_____

_____

_____

_____

How will you contact these individuals? Do you have their contact info? If not, how will you get it? When will you contact them?

_____

_____

_____

_____

Make sure you have all of the information in one space that your mock judges will need prior to contacting them. Identify dates and locations for the mock demos. Do you need approval from anyone in order to reserve the space? Use the space below to brainstorm information that your potential mock judge might need and questions that your volunteer judges may ask you.

_____

_____

_____

_____

What materials will you need for your demonstration? Create a checklist of every item.

- [ ] _____
- [ ] _____
- [ ] _____
- [ ] _____
- [ ] _____
- [ ] _____
- [ ] _____
- [ ] _____
- [ ] _____
- [ ] _____
- [ ] _____
- [ ] _____

What else do you need to keep in mind for your demonstration?

_____

_____

_____

_____

What are the worst case scenarios that you could potentially encounter?

_____

_____

_____

_____

How will you handle the worst-case scenario you identified if it were to occur so that you can use this as an opportunity to excel instead of fail?

_____

_____

_____

_____

Chapter 12

STAND OUT!

"In a crowded marketplace, fitting in is failing. In a busy marketplace, not standing out is the same as being invisible."

~ SETH GODIN

When it comes to competitive events, fitting in is failing. If your entry doesn't stand out, it will not be remembered. If it is not memorable, you will not move on to the next level. Get out of your comfort zone, exude energy, be positive (Remember? Emotions are contagious!), and connect your presentation to a topic that ignites your passion.

If you are bored while preparing your presentation, your judges will be bored while listening to it which will reflect in the scoring. Your hard work will then wind up in the boring pile—this isn't where you want to be! Do you know where that pile goes? Nowhere. Anyone can be mediocre. Strive to be dynamic.

BE BILINGUAL

Body language is a very important language when it comes to standing out (Revisit Chapter 8 for more on this). Strike a superhero pose. Keep your arms off of your chest. Don't dance. Don't play with your hair. Don't touch your face. Don't fidget. And no matter what song has been blasting in your head all week, DON'T DANCE!

YOU ARE GRAND!

Know when and where your competition is and what day. Your advisor may be judging or doing other duties, so be your own advocate.

1. First Impressions matter! Making a great first impression starts with a grand opening. Walk into the room with confidence, your head held high and prepared to give a strong handshake and greeting.
2. Make eye contact with every judge and smile at each judge.
3. Think about your competition as a book. If you want your book to get read make it look interesting and differ my then the other covers. Not just different, better. Dress the part AND make sure that any materials, manipulatives, etc are remarkable.

Stand Out by Eliciting an Emotional Response and Creating Jaw-Dropping Moments

Have you ever watched a TED Talk? The most viewed TED Talks are memorable because they are emotional. The speaker connects with the audience's emotions, whether it's through their excitement, passion, vision, or at times, empathy. This style of storytelling inspires the person to remember the talk, rewatch it, and recommend it to others. Ultimately, the goal of a TED Talk is to influence the listener to think or act differently as a result of the idea that was shared. As a competitor, you want your talk to elicit the same response as that of a TED Talk. If your judges think or act differently as a result of your presentation, you know that you've wowed them and made an impact.

One way that an emotional connection is established with the judges is through delivering wow moments that cause the judges to connect to the topic in a deeper, more richly ingrained way. According to Carmine Gallo, author of Talk Like TED, "The jaw-dropping moment—scientists call it an 'emotionally-competent stimulus'—is anything in a presentation that elicits a strong emotional response such as joy, fear, shock, or surprise. It grabs the listener's attention and is remembered long after the presentation is over."

Chris Anderson, the curator of TED, further explains that a jaw-dropping moment creates a knowledge gap that the listener then needs to fill. When the jaw-drops, we have our audience exactly where we want them, hungry to know more. So as you think about your competitive event, is there a wow moment that occurred in the conception of the idea, during the process of designing your presentation, or from the outcome itself? What emotional connections can you make with the judge and/or your audience?

I was asked to judge a public speaking event a few years ago and was mesmerized by one student in particular. She shared emotional stories of the struggles that occur in international adoptions and took us on a journey not only with the words she said but in the images that she shared as the visual backdrop. It wasn't until the very end of her presentation that she shared that one of the adoption stories she spoke of was actually her own story. The great reveal was showing the picture again of the child in China and then the image morphed into her image. She not only won the event but had every judge in tears!

When telling a personal story, keep in mind that eliciting the emotion of compassion needs to be done with care as you do not want your audience, your judges in this case, to experience compassion fatigue. Compassion fatigue is a phenomenon in which there appears to be an "indifference to the charitable appeals on behalf of those who are suffering, because of the frequency or number of such appeals."

That being said, I also urge you to be authentic and to share, but not overshare. Test your stories on trusted adults to see if the topic may be too personal for the competition that you are participating in.

The Snore Fest

Did you get tickets to the last year's Snore Fest? Right. No one did... because most people prefer to fall asleep in their own beds.

Neurologist John Medina explains that "the brain doesn't pay attention to boring things... When the brain detects an emotionally charged event, the amygdala releases dopamine into the system. Because dopamine greatly aids memory and information processing, you could say the Post-it note reads 'Remember this!"

So what does this mean for you as a competitor?

In most cases, your judges will be scoring countless entries on the same topic. Sometimes the entries begin to blur together. The only entries that win are the ones that stand out. Make sure your entry has a unique spin that distinguishes it from the other entries. Again, if you are bored creating your entry or presentation, the judges will be bored scoring your presentation.

The WOW Factor

You want the judges to remember your presentation or entry, even if they scored twenty entries before or after yours. Find ways to incorporate passion, shock, humor, excitement, or even disgust to build a connection with our judges and grab their attention.

Anticipate what your competition may be doing for their presentation, then do it differently and do it better. The more "Wow" moments you include, the more engaged the judges will be, and ultimately, the more they will remember your competition entry.

When invited to the TED stage, one of the first things that Chris Anderson and the staff review when preparing presenters, is the slide deck. Although a slide deck is not required, those giving a TED Talk are encouraged to follow a few simple, but important guidelines if using presentation software. The first rule of thumb is to get rid of excessive bullet points and wordy slides.

Too often, presenters use their slides as notes to stay on track, but in reality, the audience is reading the slide ahead of time and missing what is being said. Slides should be a backdrop to enhance the presentation. Chris Anderson also reminds presenters that there is no limit to the number of slides, so use a new slide for each thought and get rid of bullet points.

DRIVE YOUR MESSAGE HOME WITH THE POWER OF STORYTELLING

And again... it comes back to stories! Many times, the holy-smokes moment in a presentation comes in the form of a story. The most inspiring TED presenters tell stories to get their point across and to connect with the audience. Bryan Stevenson told story after story to make his talk on the TED stage personal, and to build a connection with his listeners as he shared his powerful message, "We need to talk about an injustice".

His crowd was so inspired by his emotional stories, that they raised 1.12 million dollars that night from the audience and the TED organization. There is power in sharing a persuasive narrative!

John Medina explains the power of stories in terms of brain science. Studies show a correlation in brain activity when listening to a story. A brain-to-brain coupling occurs, and when executed correctly, you are literally syncing your brain with that of your audience.

How does this apply to your competitive event? When explaining concepts that are technical, analytical, or difficult to comprehend, find a story that illustrates the information. It may be your personal story or a story that you've heard someone else share but whatever the case, make sure the story you are sharing drives your message home.

One of the TED Commandments say, "Thou shalt not murder PowerPoint." Before learning how to deliver presentations in a TED-like fashion, I was one of the worst offenders! I had a slide deck for every lesson and used the slides as my presenter notes with too many words and bullet points. Many are now on Slideshare, and I shudder to think of how many words were in one of my typical presentations.

If you are using slides in your presentation, they should be minimalistic and enhance the words you are saying. Akash Karia sums this up bluntly but powerfully in his book, *How to Design TED Worthy Presentation slides*, "If you and your slide are saying the same thing, one of you is not needed."

A jaw-dropping presentation ends with a call to action, whether the presentation is on the TED stage or competing in your CTSO event. Why does your message matter? What do you want your audience to do with your message? How will your judges look at the world around them differently? Presentation literacy is something that benefits us all when we embrace the power of our voice to spread ideas.

Captivating images are just one way to create a visually stunning presentation. By using powerful and descriptive words, presenters can create a mental image just as powerful as the images on a slide deck. Short video clips, animations, intriguing props, and demonstrations also work to make presentations dynamic. TED Talks are free to download and use as a reference. You have limitless options to incorporate compelling visuals, technology, fabrics, metals, wood materials, medical demonstrations... which all add to a more interesting presentation. Make sure this, of course, falls into your competition guidelines!

YOYO
(YOU'RE ON YOUR OWN)

What makes your entry stand out? What are some unique elements that you can add that will make your competitive event entry unforgettable?

_____

_____

_____

_____

When practicing and preparing for your event, ask for feedback as to whether portions of your entry are boring or dull. How can you jazz it up?

_____

_____

_____

_____

How can you use emotions to make your presentation more engaging?

_____

_____

_____

_____

We've talked a lot about storytelling throughout the chapters of this book. Why? Our brains are designed for stories! How can you encorporate the power of storytelling to make your presentation or entry jawdropping?

_____

_____

_____

_____

Chapter 13

PREPARE PREPARE PREPARE!

> *"My superpower is that I wake up with a ton of energy and apply it to everything I'm working on and keep doing that until I get an acceptable outcome. That, plus resilience in the face of failure. My daily mantra."*
>
> **~ FRED WILSON**

You will always wish you had started preparing earlier, so begin now! Create a competition calendar and honor it, just like you would sports practice.

EXPLORE YOUR CTSO WEBSITE

It is important to scour your CTSO event site to determine key information for your chosen competitions including membership best practices, e-magazines, webinars and tutorials, power points, videos, testimonials from previous competitors, deadlines, dress and attire expectations, date and time of the event, location and preferred hotels, key people you should be interacting with and any other additional resources that are available to CTSO members. The more you know, the further you will go!

Locate the rubric for your event and use the rubric as your checklist. I cannot emphasize this enough. I have seen some over the top, amazing projects and presentations that were mind-blowing, but they did not win first place, and sometimes didn't place at all. Why? The judges are scoring the components based on a very specific rubric. If you do a ton of extra work on components that are not included in the rubric, as judges, there's usually not a bonus section to include extra points for your hard work outside of the perimeter of the project. Many times, all of these extra areas may be diminishing areas that are on the rubric.

For example, recently I judged state entries for SkillsUSA and one of the areas that I was assigned to was Promotional Bulletin Board. One of the first entries that we judged was a masterpiece! The display itself was stunning, and the three individuals had put together a clever script that went along with the theme. The amount of practice that they put into it was evident. My heart sank when they shared a scannable QR code. They had made this extra effort, but according to the rubric, I had to deduct points as this weren't allowed to include this and they had to incur a penalty. I thought they could still survive the loss of points until they pulled out a cell phone to show us the video that they had created that was connected to the project, which was another forbidden entry, and so another deduction was added. After scoring the visuals and the verbal presentations, we went back through the entries to score the remaining components, one of which was making sure the project was within budget. Not all of the materials that were used were accounted for and the cost was still over the allotted amount, which prevented them from placing and moving on to finals.

The moral of this story is to make sure that you read your rubric, then reread it again to make sure you know exactly what is being asked of you. If you are still not sure, reach out to your advisor. Your advisor may have to contact the state director for clarification and to make sure that you are clear on the requirements and expectations. This specific directive is one of the most important, if not the most important, aspects of preparing for your event.

GUEST VOICE: DR. PATRICK A. BIGGERSTAFF

Director of CTE and Adult Education
Area 31 Career Programs
Indianapolis, IN
Twitter Handle: @BiggerstaffIN

Prepare to Succeed

Congratulations on your decision to participate in a Career and Technical Student Organization (CTSO) competitive event. If you have not competed before, you will find that the experience will help to grow your professional skills as well as your network of friends. The first step in preparing for CTSO competition is to familiarize yourself with contest rules, technical standards, and any resources required of competitors.

This information can often be found on your CTSO's competition website. Additionally, many local and digital resources can help you to boost your chances of success.

You will benefit from reviewing tests and activities from previous years, discussing strategies with former state or national competitors, and/or exploring CTSO competition strategies online. While some aspects of your event will be specific to a content area, I encourage you to peruse the general competition strategies recommended by other CTSOs. As a former DECA advisor, I know that this organization offers a host of online tips to help you show your best.

For many participants, it is not a lack of content knowledge or unfamiliarity with competition requirements that holds them back. Rather, confidence is their biggest barrier to success. Your performance will improve as you learn to communicate in a confident, organized, and professional manner. I recommend that you research topics like "communicating power and professionalism," and that you practice these skills during the months leading up to your event. If possible, I recommend that you practice at least once per week; preferably in a local competition or small group presentation format. This experience will be enhanced if you receive feedback from an authentic audience of industry professionals. If your school program does not have such a structure in place, then I would recommend that you discuss this possibility with your advisor.

Competitions are meant to be challenging. While you may not know exactly what your case or challenge will be, you can prepare for success by making the most of your preparation time. In addition to the recommendations outlined above, be sure to take advantage of your school-based opportunities. Consider the ways in which your classroom and chapter activities can help you to develop your skills and understanding. If you are able to compete with a strong skill set and a professional demeanor, then you will be likely to find success in both your competition and in life.

They Are All Going To Laugh At You

While that may feel true, unless your presentation is meant to be a comedy, that won't happen. Learning how to handle criticism begins when you are practicing by telling the mock judges exactly what he or she should be judging you on—such as to count how many times you use filler words, or if you unintentionally dance when you deliver your demo.

Once you are comfortable with being judged on what is expected of you, ask someone to heckle you during your speech. If you are truly prepared—nothing will get in the way of you delivering your message.

When constructive criticism is offered, accept it graciously. It may sting the first few times, but when you recognize that the criticism is offered only with the intention of helping you improve, you will be grateful to hear it from the mock judge instead of the actual one.

Prepare for Competition Jitters

As mentioned in chapter 7, feeling a little nervous (or extremely nervous) is good news—it means you are human! Now let's explore how to turn your nervous energy into excitement.

You will be nervous before and during your competition. Guess what, your competitors will be too! Get over the idea that you can somehow prevent them, it's part of being human, and part of caring about how you perform. How you handle your competition jitters depends in large part in how you've prepared, including how you've prepared for how to deal with nerves.

Visualize your way to success! Envision yourself performing and having an outstanding event. Even visualize yourself walking away from the event knowing that you have given it your all.

Have a mantra or quote that you can mentally repeat as you are getting ready to compete. Even something as simple as, "If it's going to be, it might as well be me" or "I've got this!" can help to replace any negative that could potentially creep in.

Assume rapport. Your judges are there as volunteers and they want you to succeed!

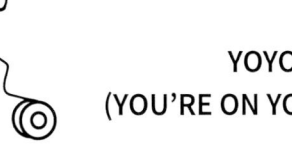

YOYO
(YOU'RE ON YOUR OWN)

In this chapter, you asked someone to heckle you during your presentation. How did you handle this disruption? Will this help you in feeling less intimidated during your presentation?

What feedback have you received during your practice sessions so far? Has the feedback been helpful? If so, were there actionable steps that you could take to improve?

What are three mantras or quotes that you will memorize and use to replace any self-doubt or negative self-talk during your competitive event?

Chapter 14

CONGRATS, YOU DID IT! NOW WHAT?

Take a moment to bask in the joy of knowing your hard work paid off! Enjoy the awards ceremony, the medal, and the accolades. Remember that you didn't get here alone—contact each person who helped you get to the moment and give them a heartfelt thank you, especially your adviser!

Once you have let your big win settle in, switch gears and start this process... all over again! You are the top, or amongst the top in your state. You are now up against the winners from every other state! NOW is when the bigger work begins.... Yep, let that settle in!

I have seen too many state winners feel that they have "arrived" after winning at the state level and instead of kicking it into, they stop. Being number one in your state in no way guarantees or prepares you to compete against all of the other number one spots out there. I've seen competitors leave nationals devastated as moments earlier they were number one, and suddenly find themselves ranking in the bottom quadrant because they stopped there.

The good news is, this isn't going to happen to you! You are reading this companion guide and know it's now time to take your competitive event to the next level.

GUEST VOICE: MARNI LANDRY

Grand Canyon University
K12 STEM Outreach Manager
Former Arizona HOSA Advisor of the Year
marni.landry@gmail.com @marni_landry

You Qualified for Nationals! Celebrate, then PANIC!

Congratulations on qualifying for nationals! I too qualified for nationals my first year advising and was lost. Luckily I had prior experience traveling with students internationally and used what I had learned to make it to nationals and back without incident. However, I was not prepared for the beast known as the HOSA International Leadership Conference.

Advisor preparation:

Plan for nationals BEFORE you qualify for nationals. If you have never traveled with your students out of state, check your district's policies on: travel requests, school board lead time, chaperone requirements, funding sources, and requisition timelines. Prepare for the cost at the beginning of the year. Find out how much your CTE department contributes (if any) to travel and registration costs. Present this to your executive board and have them include a plan in their program of work to fill the funding gap during your year of fundraisers. Depending on location, travel & hotel can cost up to $1500 per student. We did our best to cover at least half of the cost with each qualifying student paying the other half.

Send a "Save the Date" to members and parents at the beginning of the year with travel dates, add at least one day at the beginning and the end of the conference dates for travel.

Once you know who's qualified, immediately contact your district or state CTSO travel agent for travel quotes. Write a letter home to parents including these topics of explanation: payment of balance, flights, hotel, ground transportation, expenses to expect, dress code, and a packing list. Make sure the packing list is VERY specific (i.e. formal uniform, CTSO approved casual outfit, dress shoes, socks, medications, competition materials, toiletries, chargers, etc.). I have had students forget all of these items, you cannot be too specific!

Student preparation:
It can be difficult to convince a state gold medal winner that they are starting over in their competition for nationals, but they are. I have had several state medalists get to nationals and not place in the top 10 due to understudying and overconfidence. Remind students that everything starts over at nationals, and that if their competition has 2 rounds, they still have to test out of round one. This sounds obvious, but not to students; often they spend all of their time practicing round two (the skills portion) without restudying for the round one written test. Pairing your students up with other state winners in April and May is a great way to reignite their competitive fire. First, it gives them new study partners, and second, they will encounter other students who have at least the same or better skill set and knowledge base.

To make the most of the national experience, students should attend as many conference workshops as possible. Incentivizing the workshops helps to get them to attend; create a passport they get signed each time they attend a workshop, require a small summary for each workshop attended, or require a presentation to the chapter upon return. In addition, there are targeted leadership training workshop opportunities at various levels, I recommend signing up each attendee for training. You may even sign them up for an officer training workshop, even if they are not an elected officer. These students will then host a mini-workshop for the membership when they return home. This is a great way to prime someone you see as a future officer who doesn't yet know they are going to be coerced into running for office.

Finally—find an advisor who has attended nationals and ask them to share, I have never met a CTSO advisor that was unwilling to help. Please feel free to contact me for additional information, ideas, or support.

"If you're remarkable, it's likely that some people won't like you. That's part of the definition of remarkable. Nobody gets unanimous praise–ever. The best the timid can hope for is to be unnoticed. Criticism comes to those who stand out."

~ SETH GODIN, Purple Cow

Also, be prepared for the possibility that not everyone will be happy for your win. Don't let this get you down and do not let anyone steal your joy! Stand out!

YOYO
(YOU'RE ON YOUR OWN)

Woohoo, you made it! Now it's time to create a new timeline and take your competitive event entry to the top! Use the space below to determine deadlines for nationals and time that you will set aside to preparing for your next competition.

_____

_____

_____

_____

Did you receive feedback from the judges? How can you make your entry even better? Hold on… Can you make your entry better? Visit the national website and find out what the guidelines are and if there are different guidelines for nationals.

_____

_____

_____

_____

Chapter 15

DIDN'T TAKE FIRST PLACE OR ADVANCE TO NATIONALS?

"You do not equal the project. Criticism of the project is not criticism of you."

~ **SETH GODIN,** Purple Cow:
Transform Your Business by Being Remarkable

POST CONFERENCE BLUES

Participating in a competitive event is an endeavor that consumes time, energy, and sometimes, yes, sweat and tears. The months and days leading up to the event are climactic, and the CTSO state conference most likely will be one of the highlights of your middle school, high school, or even college years! It is normal to feel down after the event, even if you took first place. I refer to this as the "Post-Conference Blues". How do you feel your time now? All of the excitement and the feeling of walking on air with your friends at the conference can feel deflating after it's all done.

Since you are most likely reading this chapter prior to the conference and your competitive event, you know that the Post-Conference Blues will most likely happen and you can have a plan to offset these feelings. For example:

- Schedule an outing with a friend that you haven't spent as much time with due to your time preparing for your competitive events.
- Prior to the conference, ask your parents or guardians to make your favorite meal or snack for the evening that you get back. Enjoy the meal as a family and share all of the great memories that you made.
- Start planning for the next CTSO competition or have another sign up for another competitive event to begin training for, or, organize your own friendly competition!
- Visit www.futureme.org prior to the conference and write a letter to your future self. Schedule the letter to be delivered to your inbox on the day that you get home.

"When you take risks you learn that there will be times when you succeed and there will be times when you fail, and both are equally important."
~ ELLEN DEGENERES

WINNING AT LOSING

If you didn't win and didn't advance to nationals, you may leave the conference feeling downright dumpy. Your first reaction is to beat yourself up or think of everything that you could have done differently—congratulations, that means you are human! We are designed to react this way, and it helps us to improve moving forward.

How you handle a win OR a loss makes you a winner or a loser or can be a win or loss in and of itself. Being a good sport, and practicing how you handle a loss is going to be a life skill that will lead to future success. Life is full of disappointments, and even if you didn't win the medal, think of all that you did win:

- New skills and/or knowledge that you will be able to apply to a future job, or even next year's competition
- Deeper friendships with CTSO members who you've shared the journey with
- Regardless of whether you won a medal, your competition should be included on your resume
- Discipline and time management skills
- And on and on!

> *"True sportsmanship is… Knowing that you need your opponent because without him or her, there is no game. Acknowledging that your opponent holds the same deep-rooted aspirations and expectations as you. Knowing that, win or lose,*

you will walk off the course with pride. Always taking the high road. And always, always, always being a good sport."

~ LORII MYERS, No Excuses,
The Fit Mind-Fit Body Strategy Book

HOW TO BE A BAD LOSER

The only thing that is worse than being a bad loser is not recognizing that you are one, and thus, developing bad habits for life. Identifying how NOT to handle a loss is key to being a good loser. Here are some reactions that will not serve you well now, or in life:

- Play the victim—the judges were unfair, the event was unfair, life is unfair.
- Blame—your partner messed up, your advisor didn't prepare you, the weather was bad, your competition had better equipment, and so on.
- Play the "Ain't it Awful" game—complain to everyone who will let you bend their ear.
- Discredit the Winner—instead of allowing the winner to enjoy their victory, saying that you had a bad day or that you weren't at your top performance.
- Sulking—having a sour attitude and taking your loss out on those around you by snapping at them, or retreating and refusing to talk.
- Rage On—destroying your project, tearing apart papers, kicking that chair...

"When you complain, you make yourself a victim. Leave the situation, change the situation, or accept it. All else is madness."

~ ECKHART TOLLE

HOW TO BE GOOD AT LOSING

"We use the signals of regret and relief to update our models of the world, and this helps us navigate our choices the next time a similar situation arises."

~ DAVID EAGLEMAN

There is no way around it, when it comes to competitions, someone has to win and someone has to lose. It's easy to feel frustrated, and it's okay to mourn the loss and to talk it out with others, or even take some time to go for a walk alone and think it through. Acknowledge how you feel. Next, own the loss and determine where you can improve and raise your game.

As an FCCLA advisor, I had a student that started competing during his freshman year. It wasn't until his senior year, after three years of failed attempts, that he finally won first place in the culinary arts competition and him and his team advanced to nationals. That same year, he won the C-CAP competition and won a scholarship after placing first at the Art Institute "Chopped" competition. He didn't quit, he didn't give up, and his perseverance paid off.

Getting good at losing is a success in and of itself that will make you a winner at life. Here are just a few ways that you can handle a loss like a champ:

- Congratulate and praise your competitor.
- Own the loss. A sign of true leadership is taking responsibility instead of blaming. Yes, it is possible that the judge was unfair or that a teammate buckled under pressure. Both are outside of your circle of control. If you instead focus on your role in the loss, you will be able to grow and improve.
- What did you do well? Acknowledge your strengths and those of your partner or teammates. Build on what you did well.
- Remember your why. Why did you sign up in the first place? What are the positive outcomes that you have experienced along the way?
- Don't quit! Start preparing now for your next competition, whether it's a CTSO event, a sport, or a competition for another student organization.
- The best way to improve is to compete against people who are better than you. Find opportunities to challenge yourself by getting in over your head and take on more competitions as you prepare for future competitions.

"Even when they fail, great leaders believe in their abilities. Acknowledging and learning from mistakes allows you to lead by example, and encourages your team to see mistakes not as the end of the line, but as the beginning of growth."

~ RON GIBORI, Entrepreneur and Creative Director, Idea Booth

GUEST VOICE: TAMMY ESTES FRY, PH.D.

Teacher Education Instructor
Blue Valley Center for Advanced Professional Studies (CAPS)
@tammyfry
www.tammyestesfry.com
www.edtechgineer.com

The Importance of Being a Good Sport

Participating in competitions shows initiative. Those involved spend extra time and effort, creating a product or presentation that reflects hard work, determination, and a willingness to participate in something greater than themselves. The purpose of these events is not to rank people in an order that labels ability and potential, but rather to enhance the entrepreneurial spirit of risk-taking and collaboration necessary for success in the world outside of academia. The participants show a willingness to participate in opportunities outside of their comfort zones.

Along with any risk-taking comes the possibility of failure or loss. People often feel that by being defeated, they must face the realization that they cannot do something, or at least do it as well as others. Being a good sport is important in every competition, but it is especially important when competing in a professional environment that models itself after collaborative professional working environments. Accepting the differences and opinions of others and realizing that interpretations of their work could be subjective makes the participants stronger individuals. Do not take one loss as a descriptor of abilities or efforts. Revel in the successes of others. Jealousy and regret are the most certain characteristics for halting progress and passion.

By entering a professional competition, students are collecting experience that cannot be obtained in a textbook and makes learning more relevant to mirror the conduct of the professional world of work. Enjoying the successes of others allows one to see the path to improvement and encourages movement toward a greater goal. Participants should be encouraged to enjoy intrinsically-motivated personal steps forward, much like the "real world" in which not every success might be acknowledged but is most certainly a step toward stronger personal strength and learning. By practicing good ethics and accepting loss graciously, students are building the character necessary to become a part of a collaborative network of professionals who build others up for the good of the world around them.

YOYO
(YOU'RE ON YOUR OWN)

What is something that you can look forward to post-competition in order to offset "Post Conference Blues"?

_____

_____

_____

_____

What did you do well in your competitive event? If competing with a partner or as a team, what did they do well?

_____

_____

_____

_____

What did your competitors do well?

_____

_____

_____

_____

What do you want to work on and improve?

_____

_____

_____

_____

What's next? What competition do you want to tackle and prepare for in the near future?

_____

_____

_____

_____

What experience did you gain that will serve you well and build your repertoire?

_____

_____

_____

_____

Bonus

TOP TIPS—THE CLIFF NOTES VERSION OF ACING YOUR COMPETITIVE EVENT

Becoming skilled in any of the areas of CTSO competitive events could lead to scholarships, national competitions, and some fantastic experiences that will be welcome additions to your resumes and portfolios.

Whether you are competing in a STEM Fair, a Talent Search, or at a Career and Technical Student Organization, each may require different skill sets, but the one common denominator for all of these competitive events is that public speaking and presentation skills are crucial to winning the gold. Regardless of the content, the ability to communicate ideas effectively may be the game changer or the deal breaker and ultimately determine if you go home with a certificate of participation or you go on to compete in the nationals.

Having served as a judge for many of these organizations, I want to share some thoughts that will help you when you have your own big moment in the spotlight.

THE TOP TIPS FOR MAKING YOUR COMPETITION A SUCCESS AND DOING YOUR BEST.

1. Make a grand entrance. Walk into the room with confidence, head held high, a smile on your face, and be prepared to give a strong handshake and greeting. Remember from the moment you step into the room to make eye contact with every judge.

2. Dress for success! **"It's not about what you wear but what you accomplish"**... doesn't apply to you when you are engaging in competitive events. Success icons, such as Mark Zuckerberg, may be able to get away with his *"Every day is Friday!"* clothing choices, but he has the luxury of having already proven himself. You may be far superior to good ole Mark, but you have not been tested by fire, so you will still need to convince the judges what it is that you've accomplished. Remember the old adage: "Dress for the role you want, not the role you have.".

    First impressions definitely matter. You only get one chance to make an impression. Once you've won over your judges, the cards are stacked in your favor due to the primacy effect.

    For example, if you are competing in a culinary arts event, make sure you are dressed like a chef and your uniform meets current standards. If a business suit is more appropriate, then ensure that you pay attention to every detail. Tuck your shirt, polish your shoes, brush your hair and teeth (...it's basic hygiene people! ...*for crying out loud!*).

It doesn't take a big budget to look the part—your school may have a competition closet. If they don't, start one! There are lots of professionals in your community and surrounding neighborhoods who need an excuse to clean out their professional wardrobe for a good cause. (Tip: This could be a great community service activity for your chapter, one that leaves a legacy for years after you've left the program!). If planning your professional wardrobe on a tight budget, plan in advance and check out local thrift stores and clothing banks. This could actually be a fun excursion for you and your chapter, make an event of it! Plus, it's good for the environment—repurpose and reuse. It's good for everyone!

3. Assume rapport. Most of the judges are there to help you and want to see you succeed. (To be honest, I'm not exactly sure what the other judges are there for... but if you happen to find out—please let me know!) So rest in the idea that there are only a handful of grouches that sign up as judges. The odds are very much in your favor.

   Besides, the more relaxed you are, the more successful you are...

4. Start a TED-Ed Club at your school. This will give you and your peers a platform for developing and communicating ideas while practicing your skills at public speaking.

5. Watch this playlist to calm your nerves before your big event: Talks to watch before speaking in public: https://www.ted.com/playlists/226/before_public_speaking

6. Practice your presentation relentlessly until you can do it in your sleep. Make a commitment to practice once a day for a month and you will definitely see the difference it makes ...and so will the judges. It takes practice to appear natural! Successful speakers like Warren Buffet and Mel Robbins have often touted the importance of doing what you fear to get good at it. The more you speak in public, the more comfortable you will be.

   Oh and by the way... make the commitment to practice once a day for a month several months before your event! Most likely, you will see the need to continue this cycle in the months to come.

7. Be prepared for every possible scenario of what could go wrong and have a plan for how to overcome any challenge. As Chris Hadfield mused in his TED Talk, "There's nothing so bad that you can't make it worse."

8. Show your passion! Emotions are contagious. When a speaker is passionate about what they are talking about, it shows. It's much easier to overcome nervous energy if you believe in what you are saying.

9. And finally, have fun! If you have followed the nine recommendations above, the competition will be a joyous event instead of a stressful, or even dreadful fiasco. Again, emotions are contagious—including joy.

YOYO
(YOU'RE ON YOUR OWN)

Practice your grand entrance! Literally! Either behind closed doors or in front of family in friends. After your practice session, reflect on how you felt. Did you feel confident? Are there areas that you want to work on? Don't stop here, continue to practice strutting your stuff!

_____

_____

_____

_____

How will you dress for success? What will you wear?

_____

_____

_____

_____

What are some key takeaways from the playlist in tip five?

_____

_____

_____

_____

What are some possible worst case scenarios? What are the benefits of preparing for every worst case scenario possible?

_____

_____

_____

_____

Bonus

THE FINAL 24 HOURS BEFORE YOUR COMPETITIVE EVENT

HERE ARE SOME TIPS FOR THE FINAL 24 HOURS PRIOR TO YOUR EVENT.

1. Know the layout of the space you will be competing in.
2. Choose your outfit wisely. Sweat rings are a disaster and a missing button or unzipped zipper can certainly be a huge distraction. Make sure you choose colors that contrast (image of floating head) Also, make sure outfit is mic friendly if using a lapel.
3. Static cling (east coast)
4. Drink water. But don't over do it. It is a sitcom in the making if you need a bathroom break when the spotlight shines on you. The best idea is to drink a third of a bottle right before it's time for your competition.
5. Have your slide deck available in at least 2 places.

6. Do you have internet access? Do you have the passcode? Do you have the correct connections?
7. Arrive early, minimally an hour prior to the event. Again, you should always be planning for the unknown variables.
8. Water—tuck a bottle away under the podium drink 1/3 before going on stage
9. Do the Wonder Woman Power Pose Tony Robbins—exercise

Bonus

HINTS FOR A SUCCESSFUL COMPETITION!

ADVICE FROM THOSE THAT HAVE COMPETED BEFORE YOU...

- Start early and practice!!
- Always have confidence in yourself.
- Stay positive and self-motivated.
- Always get a decent amount of sleep, and don't stress out.
- Communicate with your peers and advisers so you can get feedback or more information on your competitive events. Also be sure to constantly practice your event, don't procrastinate!
- Be confident, know your facts, and act like you know it.
- My advice would be to simply be confident! If you believe what you are saying then so will the judges. Nobody knows the project better than you so trust yourself and just be confident with who you are.

- Be the best you that you can be.
- The advice that I have for students who are competing in a CTSO regional, state, or national competition; is to just try their best and to study as much of their area as they can. Because if they don't have the confidence or knowledge behind their area. They are not going to perform well.
- Be prepared and get everything done.
- Study and make sure you know all of the topics.
- Make sure your schedule allows time to prepare for the event.
- Before going into a performance event, always breathe! Otherwise, the judge will notice your nervousness and your anxiety just by the way you look. Also, NEVER forget to shake the judge's hand first thing! Anonomous
- Studying is definitely the key and try to find as much information about your competition beforehand.
- Practice how you play. Stay humble and hustle hard.
- Expect the unexpected
- Study hard and prepare
- Always give it your best shot.
- Don't stress! Studying and practicing will help a lot.
- Ask for help from others and to look at multiple sources to compare.
- Good luck!
- Work on public speaking before you go.
- Prepare for EVERYTHING
- Try your best and keep calm under pressure.
- Don't be nervous. Just have fun and try your best.
- STUDY EVERYTHING. Even if it may not be on your study guide or what is expected, study and memorize everything.
- Study vocabulary words, and have a good mindset.

- Be prepared.
- Try not to be nervous. Have fun. Try your best.
- Competing is a lot of work. Do things ahead of time before the competition.
- Represent your school and what you stand for when competing.
- Work hard. Don't give up.
- Pay attention and do your work.
- Good luck!
- If you can't beat them, join them.
- Keep your head and know that everything happens for a reason.
- Relax.
- Just do you.
- Relax, you know what you are doing. Pace yourself.
- Be ready and confident. You can do it.
- Practice lots, be passionate, and have fun!
- Always think outside the box. If you don't use your imagination to the fullest, you aren't going to unlock your full potential
- I would say to stay prepared and take time out to breath and relax.
- Never give up! Always do your best even on the hardest days
- Prepare as much as you possibly can!!!
- Just be calm and breathe through the competition.
- Stay confident and please practice.
- Be very confident and believe in yourself, do your best and know you do your best.
- Try to get all your jitters out and make sure you know where to go.

"Take a deep breath. You have know that you understand the content. Make sure that you practice. At least try to look at the script a few times even if you don't have time to look at the script a few days before. Confidence is key. Remember they will know if you are nervous."

~ TREVOR KRAMER, STATE OFFICER

- Be prepared with vocabulary and knowing your topic
- To study up and prepare for the competition you will be competing in.
- Give it your all and have fun!
- I would recommend that students practice communication skills beforehand and strive to dress as professionally as possible.
- I wish you good luck because it's a little rough out there!
- Don't stress and do your best.
- Do your best and compete at the best of your abilities
- Dress Formal, Be Respectful and act appropriately.
- Good luck, stay positive and don't be nervous
- try your hardest and don't give up.
- To work hard, not give up on their work and be confident about what they are doing.
- Never be afraid to be yourself. The judges only want what is best for you, which is why you should show them your passion and dedication
- Do it
- Be prepared and follow the rubric, make sure to go back even after you think you are finished and read the rubric again.

- Be confident in yourself and don't be afraid to make friends with other students from other schools at the competition.
- You don't have to be nervous or worried about anything, it's not as bad as you make it out to be.
- Go to these competitions to learn and grow.
- Find a way to study that helps you remember the information best whether it be based off of spelling, picture or color which all depends on what you are competing in.
- restudy terms at least weekly to remember them and to prepare for any potential situations.
- Get a good night's rest
- Breath
- Start early and practice!!
- Don't take yourself too seriously DURING the competition. Do take the preparation for competition seriously.
- Practice a lot! Make eye contact and use your hands to talk!

Bonus

QUESTIONS FROM PEERS LIKE YOU

1. How do I know if I am being professional or too casual?

    If in doubt, it's better to be too professional than too casual. Err on the side of dressing up. For clues as to what professional dress looks like, checkout your CTSO website. Most CTSO's have images that are examples of professional dress, along with non-examples. You may also want to look up last year's event pictures on the website and social media. What are students wearing? What are award winners wearing? Be deliberate in crafting your first impression through professional dress!

2. How do I maintain a professional appearance in a worst case scenario?

    Prior to your event, come up with every possible worst case scenario and decide how you will respond to each. By preparing for everything that could go wrong, you are able to walk into your competition knowing that you can handle anything that could potentially happen, and you've probably prevented most of these worst-case scenarios along the way.

Worst case scenarios can still happen, and can happen to anyone. Pause. Breathe. Do your best to pull the event together again. Only worry about what's in your circle of control at any given moment and do the best you can with what you have. That's truly all you can do. When a worst-case scenario happens, be graceful, smile, and handle it like a champ. If you don't win because of it, no sweat, you've still learned a valuable lesson on how to handle the sitation if it were to arise again.

At one point in my speaking career, I started writing a blog on worst-case scenarios that I have experienced with public speaking alone. Before I knew it, my blog post was long enough to be multiple chapters in a novel... and I hadn't come close to covering all of my material! (Spoiler alert, stay tuned for my next book and find out how to handle all of the mishaps that I have been fortunate to learn from!) If a worst-case scenario does occur, make the most of it, and use it as an opportunity to show who and what you are made of.

3. How do I pace my breathing?

Practice breathing. Sounds weird, huh? But it really does take practice! Our natural reaction in a stressful situation is to breathe more rapidly, or to do the exact opposite and hold our breath. Pay attention to your breathing and practice taking full breaths if you realize that our breathing is off.

4. What if the judges keep asking the same question?

   If they keep asking the same question, it could be a cue that you are not giving the response that they are looking for. You may want to try rephrasing the question and repeating it back to them to see if you are understanding what they are looking for. For example,

5. Can I compete in multiple CTSO's?

   Most likely, yes. Many competitions have a limit as to how many competitors are allowed to compete per school. Check the guidelines for your CTSO and check with your adviser. It isn't uncommon for students to be enrolled in multiple CTE classes, belong to more than one CTSO, and compete in multiple CTSO's. Like anything, it is important to maintain balance. Someone who is a member of multiple sports teams or organizations must be mindful of the commitments and stay organized. The same is true with belonging to multiple CTSO's. Anytime we say yes to one thing, we are saying no to something else—it may be that you have less time for leisurely activities or time with friends. Make sure that you have a good grasp of the time commitments that you are taking on and determine if it's manageable. You may also want to get input from parents, teachers, or trusted friends who know you and will give you honest feedback as to whether this is something worth tackling, or if it's too much.

6. Are all judges experts in the area they are judging?

Whenever possible, yes. The event organizers try to find judges who have expertise in the competitive area; however, it is sometimes difficult as competitions are typically held during the daytime when many professionals need to be at their jobs. Former students from your CTSO, college students who are volunteers, industry professionals, school board members, community members, educators who are at the district or state level, and CTSO Advisors may fill in. Whatever the case, the bottom line is this, the judges at your event are not being paid to be there and they are giving their time to do something meaningful so they certainly deserve your respect and appreciation.

7. Should I be friendly with the judges?

Are the judges your friends? Will they be? You are not there to make friends, however, you can still have a tone that is warm and inviting. I cannot say this too much—smile, make eye contact, initiate a strong handshake with each judge. Keep a professional tone that and use language that you would use when talking to your parent's friends, or your teacher's friends, not your friends.

8. Are all judges nice? Are all competitions judged fairly?

As a former EdRising State Director, I believe that in most cases, the judges we recruit are nice people and attempt to judge the competitions fairly. Most CTSO's send materials to judges in advance and have a training session prior to the competitions. That being said, I have heard of judges being rude and I know of competitions where judges didn't follow the rubric. This is rare and not the norm.

9. Where do they find the judges?

The CTSO state director and event organizers tap into several sources to find judges to volunteer for the many events. They tap into business and industry professionals that serve on advisory boards, friends, family, and community members from the industry, professional organizations, rotary clubs, alumni groups, and even former CTSO students. It isn't easy to find the number of volunteers needed, and these folks are there out of the goodness of their heart. Be sure to thank them and show your gratitude for the time that they have dedicated to help out your organization.

Bonus

AWESOME QUOTES FOR A LITTLE COMPETITION READINESS INSPIRATION

"We are what we believe we are."

~ C.S. LEWIS

"I have not failed. I've just found 10,000 ways that won't work."

~ THOMAS EDISON

"Dream big, work hard, stay humble."

~ BRAD MELTZER

"Everything you have in life can be taken from you except one thing, your freedom to choose how you will respond to the situation. This is what determines the quality of the life we've lived —not whether we've been rich or poor, famous or unknown, healthy or suffering. What determines our quality of life is how we relate to these realities, what kind of meaning we assign them, what kind of attitude we cling to about them, what state of mind we allow them to trigger."

~ VIKTOR FRANKL

"The day before something is truly a breakthrough, it's a crazy idea."

~ PETER DIAMONDIS

"Even in an organization that's doing something big and bold, there's the mundane, day-to-day execution work of keeping it going. But people need to stay connected to the boldness, to the vision, and stay plugged in to the main vein of the dream."

~ PETER DIAMANDIS

"When something is important enough, you do it even if the odds are not in your favor."

~ ELON MUSK

"I think it is possible for ordinary people to choose to be extraordinary."

~ ELON MUSK

"Your time is limited, so don't waste it living someone else's life... Stay hungry. Stay foolish."

~ STEVE JOBS

"The future belongs to those who learn more skills and combine them in creative ways."

~ ROBERT GREENE, Mastery

"Focus on what's right and do more of it."

~ JIM LUNDY

"Don't envy what people have, emulate what they did to have it."

~ TIM FARGO

30 DAY CALENDAR OF TIPS

Here are tweetable tips that you can use on social media, post on your site, or share on a calendar to give daily boosts to your members (and for yourself!). Mix and match so that the message is timely, no need to share them out in this exact order.

1. Are you ready for your CTSO Competition? In the words of Walt Disney, "Why worry? If you've done the best you can, worrying won't make it better." Ultimately, your number one goal is to be the best version of you on the big day!

2. First impressions count, so dress for success! Your attire should fit properly, be free of wrinkles, and professional in appearance. If you aren't sure if it's professional, most likely it's not... Avoid wearing trendy clothing, and keep it simple. Your attire should enhance, not distract. #CTSO #Careerteched #dressforsuccess

3. Making a great first impression starts with a grand opening. Walk into the room with confidence—head held high and prepared to give a strong handshake and greeting. Make eye

contact with every judge and smile at each judge. #CTSO #Professional

4. Dress for success! "It's not about what you wear but what you accomplish"... doesn't apply to your competitive events. Success icons such as Mark Zuckerberg may be able to get away with casual clothing, but he has already proven himself. You still have to convince your judges what it is that you've accomplished.

5. Cliche but true, first impressions matter. You only get one chance to make a bad impression. Once you've won over your judges, the cards are stacked in your favor due to the primacy effect. Dress the part. If competing in a culinary arts event, make sure your chef outfit is according to the standards. If a business suit is appropriate, ensure that you pay attention to detail. Watch Olivia Fox Cabane, The Science of First Impressions: https://www.youtube.com/watch?v=_zRZ5j2O07w&feature=youtu.be.

6. Humbleness is a virtue, but not during your #CTSO competitions! This is your time to shine! Your judges only know what you show and tell them. Be bold in sharing your accomplishments in the resume and the interview as long as you package it in a tasteful way. #CTSO #WednesdayWisdom #Careeteched

7. Assume rapport. The judges are there to help you, and in most cases, want to see you succeed. Knowing this gives you a competitive edge: More relaxed=more successful.

8. Watch this playlist to calm your nerves before your big event: Talks to watch before speaking in public https://www.ted.com/playlists/226/before_public_speaking

9. It takes practice to appear natural! Successful speakers like Warren Buffet and Joel Olsteen have discovered that you have to do what you fear a lot to get good at it. The more you speak in public, the more comfortable you will be. https://www.forbes.com/sites/carminegallo/2013/05/16/how-warren-buffett-and-joel-osteen-conquered-their-terrifying-fear-of-public-speaking/#10cf9439704a

10. Be prepared for every possible scenario of what could go wrong and have a plan for how to overcome any obstacles. As Chris Hadfield says in his TED Talk, "There's nothing so bad that you can't make it worse." https://youtu.be/Zo62S0ulqhA

11. #CTSO #CompetitionReadiness Tip of the Day: Show your passion! Emotions are contagious. When a speaker is passionate about what they are talking about, it shows. It's much easier to overcome nervous energy if you believe in what you are saying. Ramsey Musallam emulates this. https://youtu.be/YsYHqfk0X2A

12. You aced your state event and you are heading to nationals, so what's next? Practice relentlessly. Even a commitment to practice your public speaking skills once a day for a month makes a huge difference. #Careerteched #CTSO https://youtu.be/q_ccU9pBoDU

13. Do something today that your future self will thank you for on competition day!

14. Who is your competition? Who won last year's event and why did they win? How many people or teams will you be competing against? Do your homework!

15. Practice Practice Practice! Learn everything there is to know about your competition topic.

16. Ask for feedback. Let the person providing feedback know what you want them to look for (eye contact, filler words, etc) and limit it to one or two areas. #competitionreadiness #competitiveadvantage

17. "What you do today can improve all your tomorrows." ~ Ralph Marston #MondayMotivation

18. Accept the challenges so that you can feel the exhilaration of victory." George S. Patton #Careerteched #worktrends #Thursdaythoughts

19. "Believe you can and you're halfway there" Theodore Roosevelt #MondayMotivation

20. "Find a Mentor The best way to learn anything is to find someone who's doing it and learn from them. If there's something you think you want to do with your life, the best way to figure it out is to work for them and figure it out. Find that person, bring them value and I would even recommend working for them for free if you have to. You'll learn if you really want to do that thing, and if not you didn't waste years at college on it—and if you do, they can probably help you get your foot in the door." http://www.littlemight.com/high-school/

21. "Failure should be our teacher, not our undertaker. Failure is delay, not defeat. It is a temporary detour, not a dead end. Failure is something we can avoid only by saying nothing, doing nothing, and being nothing."—Denis Waitley #Thursdaythoughts

22. Ace the interview with these counterintuitive tips #worktrends #edufuture https://www.entrepreneur.com/article/301173

23. Today's Tip: Speak the language. Each CTSO/program area has a common language connected to the career field you're

preparing for. Know the lingo & jargon and use those terms! Your judges will see that you are knowledgeable & professional & this will boost your score.#CTSO #FutureReady

24. Do you have the pre-competition jitters? If so, this is good news! It means that you are A. Normal and B. you care about the competition & you are taking it seriously. Watch Amy Cuddy's #TEDTalk and practice Power Posing. Remember to fake it until you become it. #CTSO #CTEWorks #Careerteched https://www.ted.com/talks/amy_cuddy_your_body_language_shapes_who_you_are

25. Avoid procrastination! Read this blog post, and be sure to watch the embedded TED Talk by Tim Urban, "The Dark Art of Procrastination" #TEDTalks #CTE https://blog.bestself.co/productivity/time-management/the-dark-art-of-procrastination/

26. What would you do if you were not afraid of failure? I'm sure everyone here has heard that quote? But do you know the answer? Take a minute and really think about this! #Fearless #CompetitionReadiness

27. You've worked hard, you've prepared, don't throw it all away by breaking rules or making any assumptions. Reread your event guidelines. If in doubt, find out. #competitionreadiness #winningmindset

28. 13 things to do every night to feel amazing every morning #wintheday #BestSelf #WednesdayWisdom https://blog.bestself.co/productivity/daily-routines/13-things-to-do-every-night-to-feel-amazing-every-morning/

29. Start the day off right! On the day of your event, don't skip out on a solid breakfast. If you aren't competing right away, be sure to eat something an hour or two before your event. #youvegotthis #readyforit #CTSO

30. Find a Mentor. "Show me a successful individual and I'll show you someone who had real positive influences in his or her life. I don't care what you do for a living—if you do it well I'm sure there was someone cheering you on or showing the way. A mentor." Denzel Washington #CTSO #CompetitionReadiness #MentoringMatters

31. Your competitive event rubric is your guide, but how can you make your entry extra special so that it is memorable and different from every other demo the judges have seen? Stand out! #unforgettable #WOW

LINKS TO CTSO WEBSITES AND RESOURCES

- Wakelet Collection of CTSO Companion Resources https://wke.lt/w/s/K7rYXN
- CTSO Overview http://www.ctsos.org/about-us/
- Business Professionals of America https://bpa.org/
- DECA https://www.deca.org/
- SkillsUSA https://www.skillsusa.org/
- FFA https://www.ffa.org/
- FBLA https://www.fbla-pbl.org/
- HOSA http://www.hosa.org
- TSA https://tsaweb.org/
- FCCLA http://www.fcclainc.org
- Educators Rising https://www.educatorsrising.org/
- AES Education https://www.aeseducation.com/what-is-a-career-and-technical-student-organization-ctso
- ACTE CTSO Career Readiness PDF https://www.acteonline.org/wp-content/uploads/2018/03/CTSO_Career_Readiness.pdf

ACKNOWLEDGEMENTS

Special thanks to the experts who shared their experiences and expertise as "Guest Voices" throughout the book: Sam Bhat, Dr. Patrick Biggerstaff, Dr. Kevin Fleming, Cody Hayes, Dr. Marni Landry, Crissy Lauterbach, Eric Ripley, and Danny Rubin. Your expertise is invaluable in supporting students through their competition journey.

Thanks to the following students who contributed peer advice and questions to be used throughout *The CTSO Competition Companion*: Alen Miguel Serrana, Anna Kurilova, Chad Williams, Nathan Lozano, Caelum D., Lupe E., Stacey Lizarraga, Fabian Hernandez, Destiny Garcia, Martin Bode, Arin Ducharme, Daniel R., Kodi Donald Dorsey, Allison Kauffman, Karina Montes De Oca, Kayden Guenther, Stephanie Sybella Torres, Domingo Seyk-Malanche, Tyler N., Dahmare C., Cesar Feliciano, Marisol Aguilar Ojeda, Tony Galindo, Trey Williams, Alexander Blanco, Noah Fimbres, Samuel H., Gilbert A., John W., Richard Bandin, and Dasani Haywood.

Thanks to the many experts who reviewed the content of this book and provided feedback: Jenna Stone, Tim Knue, Dr. Joshua

Starr, Craig Statucki, and Dr. Katy Blatnick-Gagne. And special thanks to Adina Cucicov for the beautiful design of the cover and book layout.

And finally, I want to express my heartfelt appreciation for Michael Connet, Associate Deputy Executive Director at ACTE. Michael saw the potential of this book and worked tirelessly to support the metamorphosis of the idea into publication.